STRANGE INTELLIGENCE

Hector C. Bywater

STRANGE
INTELLIGENCE
MEMOIRS OF NAVAL SECRET SERVICE

HECTOR C. BYWATER
& H. C. FERRABY

Biteback Publishing

First published in Great Britain in 1931 by Constable & Co. Ltd.
This edition published in Great Britain in 2015 by
Biteback Publishing Ltd
Westminster Tower
3 Albert Embankment
London SE1 7SP
Copyright © Hector C. Bywater, H. C. Ferraby 1931, 2015

Hector C. Bywater and H. C. Ferraby asserted their right under the Copyright,
Designs and Patents Act 1988 to be identified as the authors of this work.

ISBN 978-1-84954-884-7

10 9 8 7 6 5 4 3 2 1

A CIP catalogue record for this book is available from the British Library.

Set in Bulmer

Printed and bound in Great Britain by
CPI Group (UK) Ltd, Croydon CR0 4YY

'Say from whence you owe this strange intelligence.'

Macbeth, Act I, Scene iii

CONTENTS

INTRODUCTION

HECTOR BYWATER WAS one of the best British secret agents operating in Germany before the First World War. Mansfield Cumming, the founder of what would become MI6, had been desperate to recruit an agent he could trust to get him intelligence on German naval preparations for war. He found him in Bywater – a 27-year-old British journalist based in Dresden who wrote on naval matters for a number of US newspapers and journals.

The first attempt at recruitment appears to have taken place in early 1910, but was initially blocked by the War Office, which was trying to protect its own agent in Germany – an Austrian who had provided good reports on Russia but, perhaps unsurprisingly, was less keen to report on German preparations for war. Cumming finally got his man more than eighteen months later, after skilfully playing naval intelligence off against the War Office.

Bywater appears in British secret service accounts as a 'fixed agent abroad', with the designation HHO, or sometimes H_2O – a typically Cumming-esque play on his name. He travelled around Germany mapping out defences and using his role as naval correspondent of the *New York Herald* as an excuse for talking his way into dockyards and naval installations in northern Germany. His experiences were written up originally in a series of anonymous articles in the *Daily Telegraph* in 1930 and, a year later, in *Strange Intelligence*, which was co-authored with the *Daily Express* journalist H. C. Ferraby.

Bywater gives one of the better descriptions of the inside of Cumming's first office, housed in part of his own apartment in Ashley Mansions, Vauxhall Bridge Road. 'The apartment, airy, is furnished as an office,' he writes:

> *Its most conspicuous feature is a huge, steel safe, painted green. The walls are adorned with large maps and charts and one picture, the latter depicting the execution of French villagers by a Prussian firing squad in the war of 1870. There are three tables, at the largest of which sits a man, grey-haired, clean-shaven, wearing a monocle. His figure inclines to stoutness, but the weather-tanned face, with its keen grey eyes, stamps him as an out-of-door man. He is, in fact, a post-captain on the retired list of the Royal Navy. Let us designate him as 'C'.*

Cumming was in fact genuinely designated 'C', initially as the first letter of his surname but eventually standing for chief – the head of the secret service. Both titles have been inherited by all of his successors in MI6, with 'C' the inspiration for Ian Fleming's 'M' in the James Bond books.

Having been recruited by Cumming, Bywater's first important mission was a visit to survey the defences on the North Sea island of Borkum, described in the series of *Daily Telegraph* articles:

On island, three hours, with crowd of trippers, but large part of it Sperrgebiet [prohibited zone], sentries with fixed bayonets and plenty of barbed wire. Persistent reports have been current that Emden is being developed as a naval base, but am unable to find any sign of this. Barracks are being enlarged, however. Borkum defended by twenty guns of various calibres, from 24cm downward, and including several 15cm high-velocity pieces on field carriages. I find in Emden a general impression that, in the event of war, Borkum will be one of the first objectives of the British fleet.

Since a scandal in which two British spies had been arrested on the island, it had been dangerous for any foreigner to visit as an individual,

But the Ausflüge [excursions] from Emden provide one with an opportunity to cross to Borkum as one of the crowd, and in comparative safety, so long as German-made clothes are worn. Next to Norderney, by Norddeutscher Lloyd Seebäderdienst steamer from Bremen. Make a careful survey of the island, and find no traces of the fortifications that had been reported as being in progress. This report came from R in Hamburg. This is not the first fairy tale he has told, and henceforth his reports will be suspect.

Bywater described how he managed to get on board the battlecruiser *Von der Tann*, which was anchored off Hamburg. 'I determined to visit her, though the risk was considerable,' he wrote, resisting any false modesty:

By a stroke of luck, I found that a local shipping man, to whom I had a letter from a mutual friend in Berlin, knew several officers of

the ship, and had visited them on board. He was going again and, by very tactful manoeuvring, I got him to invite me to accompany him. We went across in a launch, but on arriving at the ship's ladder I remarked to my companion that, being a foreigner, I might not be welcome on board. He then spoke to the officer of the watch, who was one of his friends, explained who I was (or, more strictly speaking, who he thought I was), and I was promptly invited to come up. We spent two hours in the ship, and saw nearly everything, except the inside of the gun turrets and the engine room. I memorised all the important details, and subsequently wrote an elaborate report on the ship. This was the first German battle-cruiser to be personally inspected by a British secret service man.

Unlike the *Daily Telegraph* articles, the identities of many of the British spies carrying out the missions in *Strange Intelligence* are disguised, but a number of these were carried out by Bywater himself and written up by Ferraby in a way that even Fleming would have admired.

Michael Smith
Editor of the Dialogue Espionage Classics series
April 2015

PREFACE

This book is a partial record of British secret service work in the sphere of naval investigation, not only during the Great War, but also in the critical years preceding the outbreak.

Consisting almost wholly of material now published for the first time, it throws a flood of light on a subject that has hitherto been shrouded in obscurity.

The chronicle is necessarily incomplete, for much of the truth about secret service is hidden away in official archives that are never likely to be opened. In preparing our narrative we have scrupulously refrained from divulging any information that could be considered confidential.

Although compiled solely from facts, the story unfolded in these pages will not be found lacking in dramatic interest. Were any justification needed for British secret service operations in Germany before the war, it would, we think, be furnished by this book. Those operations were, indeed, an indispensable measure of self-defence, thrust upon us by the imminence of a great national peril.

We have been at pains to respect the anonymity of the men whose methods and achievements are here described.

To the editor of the *Daily Telegraph*, our thanks are due for permission to draw upon the articles on the secret service that appeared in that journal during September 1930.

Hector C. Bywater & H. C. Ferraby

CHAPTER 1

THE HIDDEN MENACE

O N AN AUTUMN afternoon in 1910, five men were gathered round the table in the First Lord's room at the admiralty. The First Lord himself, the First and Second Sea Lords, the director of naval intelligence, and a high official from the Foreign Office formed the company. The FO man tapped a document that lay before him:

> *As you will observe, gentlemen, the paragraphs of this letter from Berlin, which I have just read to you, relate to a subject that is more within your province than ours, but the writer obviously believes them to be of importance, and as my chief shares that view, he requested me to bring them to your notice at once.*

The First Lord nodded. 'We are most grateful,' he said. 'I only wish the writer had been more explicit. May I have it for a moment? Thank you.'

He read aloud from the blue foolscap sheet, covered with the spidery handwriting that any member of the diplomatic corps would have recognised at a glance:

I was rather surprised to read the admiralty reply to those questions in the House of Commons last week as to the progress of German naval building. The information given does not tally with that which reaches me from various sources, and I have drawn the naval attaché's attention to the discrepancies. He tells me, however, that it is quite impossible for him personally to investigate the matter. He is not encouraged to visit the German dockyards, and whenever he does so he is always very carefully shepherded, and allowed to see only what his guides care to show him. Direct inquiries at the Navy Office lead nowhere. Grand Admiral von Tirpitz and his staff are bland but uncommunicative. It makes me wonder whether our admiralty people are really in touch with what is going on here.

R------, of the French embassy, told me last night that Tirpitz has lavishly financed Knapps's experiments with a new Diesel engine, which promise to revolutionise submarine propulsion. He also gave me some account of recent gunnery and torpedo exercises in the Baltic of which our naval attaché had heard nothing. He added that the Germans are undoubtedly spending money like water on various forms of naval research. All this is vague enough, I admit, but I should feel more comfortable if I could be sure that our naval people were fully informed of what our German friends are doing. I know we have a naval intelligence service, but does it extend to Germany, where it would seem to be most needed? You may perhaps think it worthwhile to pass this on to the admiralty.

The First Lord turned to the ruddy-faced sailor who sat beside him. 'What exactly is the position as regards getting news from Germany?' he inquired.

'Just this,' came the prompt answer:

We are almost entirely dependent on the naval attaché's reports and such news as Tirpitz chooses to give the German press, which is precious little. Then we get reports from L------ in Brussels, and occasionally from the two very dubious agencies in the same city, which make a business of prying into the military secrets of all the big powers and selling information to the highest bidder. The stuff I have seen from this source struck me as being highly suspicious and probably worthless. The fact is – and the director of naval intelligence will confirm this – we have no means at present of obtaining trustworthy news from Germany.

The First Lord frowned.

Isn't that rather serious? If the Germans really wanted to spring a big naval surprise on us, apparently they could do so without our having the slightest warning. It seems to me we are groping in a fog. Why is it not possible for us to organise an intelligence system in Germany?

His glance rested on the director of naval intelligence. 'Well, sir,' said that officer:

There are certain obstacles in the way. In the first place, the Cabinet, I understand, is averse from any action being taken that might give colour to the German accusation that we are encouraging espionage in their country. For some time past they have been suffering from an epidemic of spy fever, and several quite harmless British visitors have been arrested on suspicion. Secondly, the funds at our disposal are too meagre to permit of our building up a really efficient intelligence service over there. Thirdly – and this is the greatest difficulty of all – granting that we had official sanction and increased funds, we should be hard put to it to find the right kind of agents. Naval officers are out of the question. They would be marked men from the moment they crossed the German frontier. We should therefore have to employ civilians, who must not only be British subjects of good reputation, but must also have an exceptionally wide and thorough knowledge of naval affairs, particularly on the technical side. If the right type of man were found, it might be possible to put him through a course of training, to teach him what to look for and to evaluate the significance of what he saw; but all this would take time, and I, personally, think the matter has become one of great urgency.

The First Lord nodded.

Yes, I quite see the difficulties. As for official sanction, I am willing to take the responsibility of giving you that. I shall, of course, consult certain of my colleagues, but I do not think there will be any trouble when the gravity of the position has been explained to them. If any of our agents in Germany were unfortunately caught, they would, I presume, be disavowed by your department. That, I understand, is the recognised procedure in such cases.

'You may take it, sir, that His Majesty's government would not be implicated under any circumstances,' the intelligence officer assured him in a rather dry tone.

'That is quite good enough.' The First Lord rose, and chairs were pushed back from the table. The Foreign Office man accepted a Corona and took a cordial leave. The naval men drifted towards the door, but were recalled by their political chief.

'Just a moment, please,' he said. 'I hope everything possible will be done to repair the deficiency in our intelligence service we have just discussed, and I would like to be kept apprised of any progress that is made – but,' he paused significantly, 'unofficially, you understand?'

'Perfectly,' murmured the First Sea Lord.

Out in the corridor he took the intelligence officer by the arm. 'Come to my room and talk it over. I have an idea, and I believe you have something up your sleeve, too.'

*   *   *

The next scene takes place twelve months later.

It is laid in a room on the upper floor of one of those imposing blocks of residential flats overlooking the Thames Embankment, which commemorate the misguided genius of Mr Jabez Balfour. The apartment, large and airy, is furnished as an office. Its most conspicuous feature is a huge steel safe, painted green. The walls are adorned with large maps and charts and one picture – depicting the execution of a group of French villagers by a Prussian firing squad in the war of 1870.

There are three tables, at the largest of which sits an elderly man, grey-haired, clean-shaven, wearing a monocle. His figure inclines to stoutness, but the weather-tanned face, with its keen grey eyes, stamps him as an out-of-door man. He is, in fact, a post-captain on the retired list of the Royal Navy. Let us designate him as 'C'.

At a smaller table is seated a very different figure.

Tall, spare and dark, with aquiline features, his soldierly bearing betrays him for what he is – an officer of the Regular Army. This is 'F', perhaps the most capable intelligence officer of his generation. He is a linguist of the first order, his mind is a storehouse of naval and military knowledge, and his memory rivals that of 'Datas'. Against his inclination, 'F' was seconded to the intelligence service from a Highland regiment some years before the time of which we are writing. It was put to him as a matter of duty, and he knew no other mistress.

The third occupant of the room is 'C''s secretary, an incorrigibly cheerful soul who works fourteen hours a day for the pittance that a grateful country bestows on its devoted civil servants in the humbler grades.

This room is the clearing-house that deals with all despatches and reports that refer in any way to the naval armaments of foreign powers. Here they are subjected to expert scrutiny, which, more often than not, discovers fiction masquerading in the circumstantial guise of fact. No report, from whatever source it may come, is accepted at face value, for the most conscientious agent is sometimes deceived; while to agents less scrupulous the temptation to concoct news when the supply of genuine data fails is sometimes irresistible. It is of the utmost importance that counterfeit information should be detected in the first instance, since otherwise it may well mislead our naval authorities on matters of vital moment, to the grave detriment of the national interests. Moreover, the funds available for intelligence purposes are much too limited to allow any margin for waste. In the case of 'freelance' agents, payment is made on the basis of results, and no money changes hands until the intelligence department (ID) experts are satisfied that full value has been received.

Nor is it only against the dishonest purveyor of information that the ID scrutineers have to be on their guard. There are subtle brains at work in the intelligence bureaux of foreign admiralties, and these are not infrequently invoked to draw a red herring across the trail. Spurious diagrams of new warships, bearing all the signs of official origin, faked maps of fortified coastal areas, and even 'highly confidential' textbooks purporting to give details of guns, torpedoes, and signalling codes – all these were carefully prepared and circulated for the express purpose of hoodwinking the British Admiralty. A silent duel of wits between the most highly skilled experts on both sides was thus always in progress. Occasionally, of course, we got the worst of it, but on balance the British ID men more than held their own, as will be demonstrated in a later chapter.

The silence in the room is broken by 'C', who looks up from the papers over which he has been poring for the past hour.

'There's no doubt about it,' he exclaims:

This stuff from 'X' is absolutely genuine. I have checked it with every scrap of information we have got. The details we knew to be correct are repeated both in his map and in the report, while practically every item we were doubtful about is either omitted or given in a different version. I'll stake my reputation that 'X' has delivered the goods this time. If so, Borkum is not half such a tough nut as we've always been led to believe.

His subordinate walked over to the chief's desk and looked at the papers.

That's just what I told them across the road two years ago, you remember, sir? When I was at Emden I could find no trace of any really heavy stuff having been shipped to Borkum, and Moller, who used to send us in good reports from Delfzyl, always swore the 28-cm howitzers were the biggest guns on the island. 'X' repeats this, and also mentions the 10.5-cm mobile guns for which we suspected those new roads were being made.

He picked up the map that had so intrigued his chief. Drawn by an unpractised hand, it nevertheless showed very clearly all the salient features of Borkum, that small island off the Friesland coast, which, at the time of which we are writing, was regarded, rightly or wrongly, as one of the strategical key positions of the North Sea. That the seizure of this island by a *coup de main,* immediately after the outbreak of hostilities, was an essential part of Lord Fisher's plans for dealing with the German menace, is now common knowledge. Germany herself, foreseeing this rather obvious opening gambit, had begun to fortify Borkum in 1909.

The sketch map prepared by 'X' showed the site of each battery, with the number and calibre of its guns; the location of all magazines, bomb-proof shelters, and observation posts; the positions prepared amidst the sand dunes for the mobile 4.1-inch high-velocity guns, which were to supplement the fixed defences, and the narrow-gauge railway and paved roads that had been made for the transport of troops and material. Other details indicated were the main and emergency wireless stations, the secret telegraph and telephone cables leading from garrison headquarters to the mainland – as distinct from the ocean cable lines that traverse Borkum – and, indeed, every feature of the entire defensive system. Accompanying the map was a long report on the arrangements made by the German military authorities for reinforcing the garrison of the island at short notice by despatching troops and war material from Emden.

While this was considered by the ID people the best piece of work that had been done by 'X' during the first eight months of his intelligence activities in Germany, he had been highly commended on previous occasions for the accuracy and completeness of his reports. These had dealt with, *inter alia*, the progress of naval construction at the principal German shipbuilding yards, new defences on the North Sea and Baltic coasts, and recent developments in guns and torpedoes. Only rarely did 'X' guarantee the absolute accuracy of his information, yet in the main it was subsequently verified and passed as reliable by admiralty experts. Thus, for eight months our authorities had been kept well in touch with all important naval developments in Germany, and there seemed every prospect of still better results when 'X' had warmed to his work. Also, there were other agents from whom useful reports had been received.

No longer, therefore, were we groping in a dense fog. Much remained hidden from our ken, it is true; but the screen that surrounded the German dockyards and arsenals had been pierced in several places, and the glimpses thus vouchsafed enabled us to form a pretty clear impression of the whole scene.

To the post-war generation 'the German naval menace' is a

phrase of little meaning, recalling at most a page of semi-ancient history. Twenty years ago, however, it possessed a very real and sinister significance. For more than a decade, Germany had been enlarging her fleet, at first by gradual stages, but latterly at ever-quickening *tempo*. An immense war armada was being created, for an ultimate purpose of which there was never any serious doubt. The building of this fleet could only be construed as an overt challenge to the maritime supremacy of Great Britain, and for at least five years preceding the war it was accepted as such by all our national leaders, save for a purblind minority who chose to ignore the most positive and conclusive testimony. As far back as 1900, when Germany's first ambitious naval programme was launched on the crest of a wave of Anglophobe propaganda, Admiral von Tirpitz made candid avowal of its aim. In the preamble to his bill he enunciated the doctrine that Germany needed a fleet of such dimensions as would command the respect of 'the mightiest naval power', the more so in that this power, having vital interests to protect overseas, would at no time be in a position to concentrate its strength in European waters. Therefore – and the implication was as clear as words could make it – the projected German battle fleet would have more than a sporting chance of defeating the strongest British force ever likely to be encountered in the North Sea.

Passing over the intervening years, each of which brought fresh evidence of Germany's fixed resolve to try conclusions with us at her own appointed time, we come to the position that existed in 1910. By that time, Germany had recovered from the temporary setback her naval policy had met with by reason of Britain's adoption of the dreadnought type of battleship. To Germany, indeed, the advent of the all-big-gun ship was a stroke of great good fortune. By reducing all previous battleships to obsolescence it wiped out Britain's crushing preponderance in this type, and enabled Germany to start level with us in the new building race. As an earnest of her determination she rebuilt the Kiel Canal at stupendous cost to make it navigable for her new mastodons.

Before the dreadnought era, no particular secrecy was observed by any of the powers in regard to their naval preparations. Comparatively full details of new ships were released well in advance of their completion, and not seldom before their keel plates had been laid. Germany was not less communicative than her neighbours, as a glance at the naval textbooks of that period will reveal. But with the construction of the *Dreadnought* all this was changed. Anxious to keep the secrets of his 'wonder ship', Lord Fisher imposed a ban on the publication of technical naval data that had heretofore been freely imparted to the press. Thus the 'hush hush' policy was first introduced by Great Britain, and not, as is commonly believed, by Germany.

But Germany, as was her unquestioned right, promptly retaliated by imposing a censorship that was soon proved to be much stricter and more watertight than our own. British journals, unaccustomed to, and possibly resentful of, any suggestion of official control over news, continued to print a great deal of information about new warships and other naval developments occurring in this country. The German authorities, wielding more arbitrary powers, were able virtually to muzzle their own press on this particular subject. Thus the 'hush' policy recoiled on the heads of its authors, for while it failed in its purpose of denying to the Germans important information about the British Navy, it enabled them to conceal their own preparations behind a veil of secrecy, which, as we have seen, defied penetration for a number of years.

And it was precisely during this period that German naval technique was achieving its most formidable results. Revolutionary changes were taking place in the design and construction of German fighting craft; a thoroughly efficient and reliable type of submarine had been evolved after years of painstaking research and experiment; new methods of inter-fleet signalling, both wireless and visual – destined to demonstrate their amazing efficiency at the Battle of Jutland – were being introduced; new guns, new armour-piercing projectiles, new torpedoes, new mines and new explosives were in process of trial or adoption. Between 1906 and 1910 the combatant power of the German fleet may be said to have doubled, less by the increment in ship tonnage than by the improvements made in individual ships and their equipment.

Yet throughout this critical period we were receiving only the scantiest naval intelligence from Germany, and much of this was contradictory. Although we knew that a deadly weapon was being forged for eventual use against ourselves, ignorance of the characteristics and power of that weapon handicapped our efforts to devise a sure means of defence against its assault. To cite a case in point: had we obtained in advance full particulars of the Germany battlecruisers, it is extremely improbable that we should have built such 'replies' as the *Indefatigable*s or the *Lion*s. Again, had we known the extraordinary potency of the new German shells, torpedoes, and mines, we should perhaps have devoted much more attention to the armour and underwater protection of our capital ships. The word 'perhaps' is used advisedly, for, as will in due course appear, our naval authorities were, in fact, apprised of many of these Germany innovations in ample time for counter-measures to be taken before the outbreak of war. Why such measures were not taken has never been satisfactorily explained.

It is not too much to say that the reports furnished to the intelligence department by 'X' gave our authorities their first insight into the internal mechanism of the German naval machine. Previously they could see the wood without being able to distinguish the trees. Yet in such a case detailed knowledge is of paramount importance. It was not enough for our purpose to know that Germany had laid down a new battleship of such-and-such a tonnage. To build a ship that should effectually surpass the German vessel in all-round fighting power it was necessary for us to learn her speed, radius of action and armament, the thickness and distribution of her armour plating, the method and extent of her underwater protection, and a number of other details.

Germany, however, was not sufficiently obliging to proffer such information, and thanks to her admirable system of censorship, we were left in ignorance of many essential features of new ships, not only while they were under construction, but long after they had been commissioned. It was to remedy this most unsatisfactory and, indeed, highly dangerous state of affairs that our intelligence service had to extend its activities, one branch of which was represented by 'X'. Who, then, was this mysterious individual, whose reports, almost from the beginning, threw a flood of light on matters of vital moment that had hitherto been wrapped in the mists of obscurity?

For obvious reasons it would be improper, even after the passage of so many years, to disclose the identity of any member of the pre-war intelligence service. Let us therefore introduce 'X' not as an individual, but as a type, even though in writing of his work we have in mind a certain person. How he came to join the ranks of the service would make an intriguing story in itself, but once more, alas, the impulse to be indiscreet must be sternly repressed. Suffice it that, although a mere civilian, he had exceptional qualifications for the task he was invited to undertake.

In every country, no doubt, and in England beyond question, there exists a certain number of people who have no professional connection with naval or military affairs, but who are, nevertheless, entitled to be considered experts on such matters. We could name today at least half a dozen English civilians who have at their fingertips the most intimate knowledge of the world's navies. In some cases this knowledge is largely, if not wholly, theoretical; in others, it is fortified by practical experience obtained through personal contact with British and foreign warships and naval personnel.

Those men would be the first to ridicule the supposition that they could understudy the professional sailor as far as the practical side of his calling is concerned. They would even disclaim any qualification to pose as authorities on naval tactics – as distinct from strategy. They are simply students who have specialised in the study of the material elements of naval power, but of this particular subject their knowledge is extensive and even profound.

Let us give a few examples to illustrate the point. The prompt identification of warships at sea, whether British or foreign, is a science in itself, and one that assumes vital importance in wartime. We are well within the facts in stating that the most skilful exponents of this science are civilians. The late Fred T. Jane, founder of the widely known *Fighting Ships* annual that bears his name, could, and repeatedly did, astound the most experienced naval officers by his uncanny familiarity with the minutest details of every vessel of war that floated during his lifetime. To such a degree had he cultivated this faculty that, upon being shown at sea a squadron of ships of uniform design, he could instantly name each unit, though even to the trained eye, they seemed as alike as peas. One of Jane's diversions was the drawing up of questionnaires on the most abstruse technical minutiae of warships, guns, armour protection, and so forth, which he submitted to his naval friends for elucidation. As a rule the correct answers averaged 5 per cent, but Jane himself, confronted by a set of similar questions, was rarely at a loss for an accurate and immediate reply to every one.

Jane was probably unique but, before and since his time, there have been civilian students of naval technique whose mastery of their subject almost rivalled his own. During the Great War there was witnessed the apparent anomaly of civilians teaching naval officers how to recognise and identify enemy ships. In pre-war days the most comprehensive and detailed knowledge of the German Navy was that acquired by lay observers. Such, at least, was the testimony of intelligence officers of that period.

Now 'X' had been from boyhood a diligent student of naval affairs. Long before he went out into the world he knew almost by heart the ship tables and data published in *Brassey's Naval Annual, Jane's Fighting Ships* and other textbooks. His nearest conception of heaven was a visit to one of the royal dockyards, and on these all too rare occasions he invariably astonished and disconcerted the official guides – Metropolitan policemen as a rule – by shyly but firmly correcting the misinformation they dispensed to visitors.

As a small boy he wrote an essay on the Japanese naval victory at the Yalu, which only escaped getting into print by an editor's chance discovery of the author's tender age. In his fourteenth year his modest library was enriched by a birthday gift of H. W. Wilson's *Ironclads in Action*, by far the most informative work on modern naval warfare, which had appeared up to that time. Followed the *Wanderjahre*, which included prolonged sojourns in the United States and Canada and visits to several continental lands, including Germany, in which country he acquired the rudiments of what he considered to be one of the noblest and most expressive of modern tongues.

Still the victim of a roving disposition, his mid-twenties found him again in northern Europe, where he was destined to live through several hectic years. As at this time German sea power was on the flood tide of development, it was inevitable that 'X' should become deeply interested in the process. His specialised knowledge of warships and their equipment enabled him to appreciate the significance of much that he saw on his first casual visits to Kiel and the waterfronts of the Elbe and Weser. Moreover, since the nature of his business – which at this time had nothing to do with intelligence work – necessitated a careful reading of German periodical literature, he speedily became aware of the existence and extraordinary ramifications of Admiral von Tirpitz's propaganda system, which was being so effectively employed to stimulate public interest in the national navy. There is not the remotest doubt that this intensive propaganda was mainly responsible for the startling growth of anti-British sentiment among the Germany people.

A steady stream of literature poured from the *Nachrichten-Büro* of the Berlin Navy Office, in which Great Britain was always portrayed as an implacable enemy who would stick at nothing to frustrate Germany's hopes of commercial and colonial expansion. The whole nation was being indoctrinated with the belief that perfidious Albion was privily preparing for an unprovoked attack on the power that had already become her most dreaded trade competitor, and that only by the creation of a powerful fleet could this peril be averted.

When 'X' first settled in Germany in 1907 he was strongly biased in favour of the country and its people, from whom he had received many kindnesses on previous visits. He had also made German friends in the United States, while Carlyle's 'Frederick the Great' had given him a very sincere admiration for the qualities that had raised Prussia from political insignificance to a commanding position in the world. But it soon became clear to him that Germany, far from being animated by friendship for Britain, entertained very different sentiments and designs.

Few intelligent Englishmen who lived in Germany during the seven or eight years that preceded the war felt any doubt as to what was impending. On every hand there was abundant evidence of a bellicose spirit, coupled with more or less open preparation for war by sea and land. Yet in Britain itself a great number of people, including many in high positions, were unable or unwilling to realise the danger, and dismissed as alarmist fiction the plainest evidence of German hostility.

Having observed all these disquieting symptoms of political animus and the concrete proofs of martial preparation, 'X' conceived it his duty to bring them to the notice of the most influential people he could reach at home. In due course his manifest grasp of German naval affairs attracted attention in certain quarters, and eventually, though much against his own desire, he found himself a new but full-fledged member of the British secret service.

The succeeding chapters, which deal with the adventures and vicissitudes of 'X' and his co-workers in central Europe, will, it is hoped, serve to dispel many of the illusions in regard to this work, which have been created by sensational but over-imaginative writers who have no personal knowledge of their subject. We may claim, indeed, that these pages disclose for the first time the truth about the naval branch of the secret service, before and during the war. And it will be found, we think, that the wildest flights of fiction are less strange and less thrilling than the truth.

CHAPTER 2

THE MEN WHO
DID THE WORK

N O ONE CAN appreciate the work of the intelligence
men stationed abroad in the period of deep secrecy
that marked the last five years before the war without some knowledge of the extremely technical information
that they had to gather.

No useful purpose would have been served by sending in
reports that a new battleship was going to be called the *Kaiser,* or that 200 extra hands had been put to work on the
new cruiser *Emden,* or that two new submarines would be
laid down on 1 March. That kind of thing was the province
of the newspaper correspondent, far more than that of the
intelligence man. The latter's business was to find out what
technical novelties or developments were included in the battleship, what mechanical innovations were being embodied

in the submarine, or what engine-room improvements characterised the cruiser.

The newspaper correspondent could not have sent this sort of information to his paper – or, if he did, he would have been very speedily invited to leave the country. And the invitation would have been one he could not well refuse.

A good idea of the brand of technical knowledge with which the intelligence men had to be equipped can be gathered from the very interesting discussion that broke out after the war between Sir Eustace Tennyson d'Eyncourt, who was director of naval construction at the admiralty, and Dr Bürkner, who held a corresponding position in Berlin as chief of the shipbuilding division of the *Marineamt*.

Sir Eustace, after he had visited the interned German ships at Scapa Flow and carefully examined them, presented a commentary on their designs to the Institution of Naval Architects.

Dr Bürkner, in reply, published lengthy comments in the German technical paper *Schiffbau* (shipbuilding). We may take a few of his disclosures about German design as indicating the abstruse technical details for which our intelligence men had to search.

In claiming for Germany the rank of pioneer in the development of underwater protection, Dr Bürkner gave some new and interesting particulars of what had been done in this direction before the war. As early as 1905 experiments were initiated to determine the best method of protecting a ship's vitals against attack below water, and these were continued up to the outbreak of war. They involved the use of explosives against various models, including a huge floating target of 1,700 tonnes.

'We never heard that any other navy went in for similar experiments on a corresponding scale,' he comments.

In ships of the British Navy underwater protection is provided by the 'bulge'. Much of the bulging has been done since the war. The German ships built before the war had an 'outer torpedo bulkhead' and Dr Bürkner claimed that this gave greater protection than the British system because, in order to reduce the resistance to the water, the bulge has to be fined down considerably at the extremities. Of the German ships equipped with the bulkhead system of sub-surface protection, only the *Blücher* was sunk by torpedo. Nine others were damaged by underwater attack (mine or torpedo), but all survived.

This bulkhead idea, or the sub-division of the ship into many watertight compartments, has been much discussed since the war. Sir Eustace d'Eyncourt, in his paper before the Institute of Naval Architects, said that the *Baden* and most of the more recent German capital ships were sub-divided more minutely than the British in some parts, but less so in others, so that the arrangement as a whole did not make for any greater safety than in the case of the British ships.

To this Dr Bürkner replied that, since the plans of the *Queen Elizabeth* and *Royal Sovereign* classes were unknown to him, he could not express an opinion about them, but as regards the earlier ships, he was able to give a comparison of the sub-division of the rival types, based on plans of the *Emperor of India* and *Princess Royal* that fell into German hands during the war. (An interesting disclosure, that, of a success for the enemy intelligence service.)

He contrasted them in a tabular statement with the *König* and *Derfflinger,* ships of corresponding size and date.

This table shows that the number of small compartments (double bottom, passages, etc.) was practically the same in the British and German ships.

SUB-DIVISION BELOW THE ARMOUR DECK GIVEN IN PERCENTAGES OF TOTAL SPACE

	König	E. of I.	Derfflinger	P. Royal
Small compartments (less than 300 cbm)	75	70	65	49
Medium compartments (300 to 1,000 cbm)	25	7	28	9
Large compartments (more than 1,000 cbm)	0	23	7	44

While, however, the German ships had many more medium compartments but practically no large ones, in the British ships the large compartments occupied from one-quarter to one-half of the total space below water.

Dr Bürkner points out that if damage to the armour deck of the *Princess Royal* caused one of the main engine rooms and its adjoining wing compartments to be flooded, the ship would assume a list of 15 degrees, whereas corresponding damage in the *Derfflinger* would produce a heel of only 9.5 degrees. In actual fact we know that the *Derfflinger* was so damaged at Jutland that she took in 3,400 tonnes of water, and yet remained in the fighting line and got home again after the battle.

Incidentally, Dr Bürkner is among those who deny the truth of the story, first told by Lord Fisher, that the German secret service was tricked by the British counter-espionage over the design of our first battlecruisers. Lord Fisher's story was that he had caused faked plans to be prepared, and carefully planted them, a section at a time, with known German agents in Britain, these plans considerably under-estimating the actual strength of the ships that we were building. And he claimed that, misled by the bogus drawings, the Germans built the *Blücher;* thinking she was an adequate reply to our ships.

Dr Bürkner, in his article in 'Schiffbau', said:

> *The ship was in no sense a reply to the* Invincible, *for England's decision to build dreadnought cruisers was known in Germany only when work had progressed so far that her armament and leading dimensions could not be modified.* Blücher *was simply a later development of the* Scharnhorst *class and, within the limits of the design, a very successful ship. Her armour was far more extensive and no less thick – on the belt it was actually thicker than that of the* Invincible, *and her underwater protection was not limited to the magazine spaces, as in the British ship, but was continued in way of all vital parts.*
>
> Blücher *had also a 5.9-inch secondary armament, which the* Invincible *lacked, and her maximum speed of 25.8 knots, practically the same as the* Invincible's *made her the fastest large reciprocating-engined vessel in the world. The real, though belated, reply to the* Invincible *was the* Von der Tann, *and the Battle of Jutland proved the 'reply' to be quite satisfactory.*

If British comment may be allowed on this point, it may be said that the *Blücher* was probably the best and most powerful armoured cruiser (as opposed to battlecruiser) ever built.

The hammering she took at the Dogger Bank before going to the bottom revealed the staunchness of her protection.

British and German designs did, of course, follow each other pretty closely in those days, but Dr Bürkner challenged Sir Eustace d'Eyncourt's statement that the *Baden*, the last German battleship to be built, was designed as soon as Germany heard of the *Queen Elizabeth* class, of which, he said, the *Baden* was a 'fairly close, but inferior copy'.

'That is a myth', Dr Bürkner declared:

> *Except in the calibre and disposition of her guns, and in the general arrangement of her external armour, the* Baden *exemplifies totally different ideas of construction. In point of fact, not even in respect of her artillery can we admit her to be a copy of the* Queen Elizabeth, *for the calibre and arrangement of her guns were approved by the Kaiser on 6 January 1912, after endless discussion, and at that time no news as to the* Queen Elizabeth *had reached Germany beyond a rumour that a heavier British gun than the 13.5-inch was contemplated.*

In parentheses it may be pointed out here that this statement puts Dr Bürkner in a dilemma. Either he implies that the German secret service was ineffective, or else he is saying something that is not strictly true. The plans of the *Queen Elizabeth* class were drawn in 1910. The ship was on the stocks in 1912. If by that time the German secret service had not discovered something more than 'a rumour' about bigger guns, it was far less efficient than even those who were battling against it supposed it to be!

He seems to realise this danger, because in the next sentence he goes on to say:

Surely Sir Eustace does not suppose that we had knowledge of the
Queen Elizabeth*'s armament, etc., nine months before she was*
laid down?

The Baden *class was, in truth, developed out of the* König
class in all essential features except armament, and the latter
was decided on in the first days of 1912.

Dr Bürkner contends, on the other hand, that the armour protection of the *Queen Elizabeth* was modelled after that of the German *Kaiser* class, which had been begun at the end of 1909; and, further, that we adopted German ideas in restoring the 6-inch secondary armament in the *Iron Duke* and later types.

He deals next with the statement that the *Baden's* speed was inferior to that of the *Queen Elizabeth* and her protection inferior to that of the *Royal Sovereign.* As regards protection he writes:

The Royal Sovereign *is inferior to the* Baden *in defence above and*
below water excepting only the 2-inch armour deck in the citadel,
and even this deck would offer small resistance to armour-piercing
shell with good delay-action fuses, owing to its high position, pro-
nounced slope, and want of coal protection.

The corresponding arrangement in the Baden *consists of a*
1.1-inch steel deck, a 1.1-inch and 3-inch splinter bulkhead, and
bunkers filled with coal.

Sir Eustace mentions that the Baden *steamed 3 knots less on*
trial than the Queen Elizabeth, *and that she suffers from the*
drawback of mixed boiler firing. The creation of a fast battleship
division had been repeatedly discussed in Germany, and was a
pet idea of the Kaiser's, but it had been dropped at the time when
the Baden *was designed. Unless we had sacrificed fighting power*

or increased the dimensions beyond the permissible limit, it could only have been realised by adopting oil fuel only, and this was objectionable on two grounds: first, because it was impossible to guarantee an adequate supply in wartime; secondly, because coal afforded excellent protection against shell fire, mines, and torpedoes, whereas oil fuel required protection itself.

Consequently, we contented ourselves in the Baden's *case with a speed no higher than that of the preceding* König *class.*

It is to be hoped that readers will not have skipped all this technical material, which, by the way, is not nearly so technical as much that could have been put in to serve the same purpose. But it is important to realise that the work of discovering what was in progress behind the scenes could not be done by any untrained volunteer who simply had an itch for adventure.

The useful intelligence man had a fund of knowledge about engineering in all its aspects. He knew a great deal about gunnery. He had a practical knowledge of electricity. He was grounded in naval architecture and familiar with the problems of ship forms and the resistance of water to propeller thrust. He was not ignorant of metallurgy, and he had more than a bowing acquaintance with optics. Moreover, in the last years before the war he had to master the technicalities of wireless, which was then developing rapidly.

And having all that knowledge, he had to be very careful that none of the German naval authorities suspected him of knowing much about any of those subjects!

He had to play the simpleton if the conversation ever turned on technical subjects, and he had to swallow the most outrageous inaccuracies without a blink of an eyelid. He never knew what trap there might be in the apparently innocent chatter.

Some of our intelligence men were extraordinarily good actors. There was one character who was known to the inner circle as the 'Hunting Parson', though his name never appeared in *Crockford's Clerical Directory*, nor ever will. He was one of the wonders of our intelligence service, with his bawdy comic songs, his hunting crop, his brick-red neck, and his voice of a bull of Bashan.

He did splendid work in southern waters during the war. Here is a description of him and his methods, by a man who met him out there:

> *It was a breathlessly hot night in the last summer of the war. There were a dozen of us in his room, of five different nationalities – six, if you count the Scottish journalist. We were not all intelligence men, that goes without saying; but every man in that room was a trained student of international politics. And yet not one of us had a tenth part the knowledge that lay behind the apparently vacuous, happy-go-lucky countenance of our host. There was no other man in Europe, I believe, who had as much secret knowledge of the currents, cross-currents, and under-currents of international life in the area he had to watch without seeming to watch. His reports were always accurate, down to the last detail.*
>
> *And he sat at the piano that night, with a tumbler twice the normal size on a stand beside him, full of whisky and soda. He bawled his risqué songs in a cracked baritone to his own vamped accompaniment, and had us all in fits of laughter.*
>
> *But he did not touch his drink all the evening.*
>
> *Our glasses he filled time and again; his own drink he spilled surreptitiously at intervals into a wide bowl of flowers.*
>
> *I knew, because I was a trained watcher, and I watched. But I don't believe another soul in the room spotted it.*

As we came away and walked to our respective hotels when the night was far advanced, a young foreign officer who was in his own country's intelligence service accompanied me.

'Good chap, X------', he said cheerfully, as we meandered along the moonlit street. 'Good company and, like all you English, quite mad. But, my God, what a fool to drink whisky as he does, in this climate!'

That incident served to show how useful it can be for an intelligence man to build up a certain reputation.

There were plenty of men willing to do secret service work, of course. There was, from the outside point of view, a glamour, an air of romance and adventure about the whole idea, which led dozens of young men to think they would like to try their hand at it. Dozens of them were rejected simply because they had not the necessary technical knowledge to enable them to pick up useful information, or to check what they did gather for accuracy and reliability. Dozens more were rejected because they had not the right temperament.

Secret service work before the war was not romantic to the men who were doing it. No doubt, looking back after the lapse of years, those who survive may find food for laughter in some incidents they recall. There were hair-raising moments, which are better regarded from a distance than from the storm centre. There was the continuous stimulus of pitting one's wits single-handed against a great organisation.

But in actual practice the work was often dull enough and discouraging enough. There were plenty of failures. Months of hard slogging and patient research would suddenly be found to be wasted. Many an absolutely blank wall was encountered, through which no wits could find a way.

And it was a lonely life. More than one intelligence man was separated from his family for two or three years at a time. Most of the volunteers imagined that it was a job for a week or two, a sort of raid into 'enemy territory' and a dash back to safety. It was not. The good intelligence man had to dig himself in and stick it, bearing loneliness and fear and excitement and triumph in complete silence. There was not a soul he could talk to about the work, not a soul to whom he could go for advice if he was doubtful. He might, perhaps, know the name of one or two other men who were doing the work also, but he did not foregather with them, or indeed get into direct touch with them in any way. His whole life had to be self-contained. He had to cover his own tracks and take the utmost care not to uncover anyone else's.

Strong nerves were needed to stand the strain. 'The strong silent man' of the lady novelists was the right type, and even he cracked occasionally and had to be rested.

CHAPTER 3

WHILE GERMANY
PREPARED FOR WAR

BEFORE THE WAR the secret service budget of Great Britain was very considerably smaller than that of any other of the great powers. Precise figures are not available, but, roughly speaking, Germany was spending six times as much money as this country on that branch of intelligence work that was concerned with the discovery of the military secrets of neighbouring states.

Without proposing to discuss at length the ethics of such activities when conducted in time of peace, we feel it necessary to attempt to differentiate between secret service or intelligence operations on the one hand, and downright espionage on the other. The intelligence agent is in much the same position as a newspaper reporter, in that he is generally trying to procure information that the other side in unwilling to divulge. In both cases the work involves not merely the collection of basic facts, but also their analysis and logical amplification by methods of deduction. In intelligence as in newspaper work, some of the most brilliant coups have been achieved by the shrewd appreciation and collation of isolated facts, which, taken by themselves, appeared at first sight to possess only minor significance.

There can be no question as to the moral right of the state to keep a vigilant eye on the military preparations of any foreign power for which there are reasonable grounds to suspect them to be a potential enemy.

In pre-war days Germany ranked first in that category. In her case, indeed, it was a matter of certainty rather than suspicion. Apart from her intensive naval activities, the object of which was unmistakable, German agents swarmed into this country for the sole purpose of prying into our maritime defences.

During the period from 1908 to the outbreak of war, for every agent we had in central Europe there were five or six German emissaries in Great Britain. These figures apply only to professionals. Were amateurs to be included, the ratio of German to British would be ten to one.

The German methods were on the whole unimaginative, clumsy, and ineffective, involving a great deal of pseudo-espionage and very little analysis or deduction. As related in a subsequent chapter, German secret service reports sent out from England were intercepted and read by our security service over a long period preceding the war, and it was to us a constant source of amazement that the Berlin authorities should be wasting large sums of money on information that was mainly worthless. Many of these reports were so patently inaccurate that only a modicum of technical knowledge was needed to expose their spurious character. Yet the fact that those who composed them remained on the ID pay roll of the German Navy Office is proof that either the reports or, at any rate, the senders were taken seriously in that quarter.

So far as can be ascertained, Germany appointed her secret agents without setting much store by their qualifications for the work. The spies whom she planted in our naval ports and military centres were a nondescript crowd – small tradesmen, commercial travellers, 'commission agents', and so forth, whose knowledge of the highly technical matters they were expected to probe was rudimentary to a degree. Herr Steinhauer – self-styled 'the Kaiser's master spy' – who claims to have been responsible for the recruitment of this Falstaffian regiment, himself betrays in his book a very superficial knowledge of naval technicalities.

Most, if not all, of his men were professionals only in the sense that they were drawing pay. They were unskilled hands, engaged on a task that demanded highly skilled workers. Small wonder, then, that the German naval attaché in London once declared, almost publicly, that for sound intelligence work one Englishman was worth ten of his own compatriots. Others would seem to have shared this opinion long before his time, for we find Herr Lüdecke writing in his book on espionage: 'Among the secret agents of Richelieu and his successor, Mazarin, the best were generally Englishmen, whose task it was to unravel the dark intrigues of foreign courts and cabinets.'

Distinct from Steinhauer's band of permanent agents, and much more dangerous, were the numerous German naval officers who were granted special leave for intelligence work in Great Britain.

Before the war there was practically no control over visitors to the royal dockyards. Anyone could walk in, either alone or with the usual crowd of sightseers, and, once inside, it was a perfectly simple matter to 'get lost.' To enter with the crowd had this advantage, that it enabled one to go on board ships without risk of challenge, and both in the yard itself and on board any new man-of-war the skilled observer could always pick up valuable information. We are personally acquainted with several officers of the old German Navy who were familiar with every hole and corner of every royal dockyard in the United Kingdom, and who also made periodical visits to the Tyne, the Clyde, and other districts where naval construction was in hand.

A walking stick notched with inches or centimetres was useful in determining the thickness of armour plates that lay about the wharves, each plate bearing the name of the new ship for which it was intended.

The capacity of coal dumps and oil tanks could be readily estimated by the trained eye. New ships and details thereof, instruments, gun sights, gun-breech mechanisms, and a hundred other items of which a pictorial record was desired, could be snapped by a miniature camera, small enough to be hidden in the palm of the hand.

Even warships under construction and not yet launched could be, and often were, inspected and photographed. The *Queen Elizabeth,* our first 15-inch gun, oil-burning battleship, was built at Portsmouth under conditions of elaborate secrecy, the admiralty being particularly anxious to conceal the hull lines of this high-speed vessel. As a precautionary measure, taken on the eve of the launching ceremony in October 1913, the old battleship *Zealandia* was moored athwart the slipway on which the *Queen Elizabeth* was lying, thus shutting out any view of the shapely hull from boats passing up or down the harbour. Yet this did not prevent a German naval officer from obtaining a close-up view and several snapshots of the *Queen Elizabeth* by the simple expedient of going on board the *Zealandia* and asking for one of her officers whom he knew to be ashore.

As a sidelight on the futility of the ' hush' methods practised in this country may be mentioned the fact that in *Nauticus*, the semi-official German naval yearbook for 1914, there appeared drawings and a description of the *Queen Elizabeth* that were correct almost to the smallest detail, the distribution and thickness of the armour plating being shown with great accuracy. Yet this book was published only two months after the launch of the ship.

Again, while the belt-armour thickness of HMS *Invincible* and her sister battlecruisers was always given as 7 inches in British textbooks, *Nauticus*, the *Taschenbuch der Kriegsflotten*, and other German annuals gave from the first the correct figure, viz. 6 inches.

It is a safe assumption that most of the really useful information reaching the Berlin Navy Office came from its own officers, who had been on furlough in Great Britain.

This, however, does not alter the fact that reliance was placed chiefly on the permanent espionage system that had been established in this country. When we, on our side, set up a naval intelligence organisation in Germany, we were only following her example, though belatedly, and on a smaller scale.

We, too, had amateur helpers, but they received little official encouragement. From time to time officers who had been on leave in Germany brought back scraps of news that proved to be valuable, and, in one case, a British civilian visiting Hamburg picked up a clue that, on being followed up by one of our professional agents, brought us some very useful data of the arrangements for equipping and supplying German commerce raiders in wartime.

These, however, were exceptional instances. In direct contrast to German experience, nine-tenths of the really sound and helpful information that came to intelligence department (ID) headquarters in London was gathered by our permanent agents, whose reports, collated in chronological order, would give a very complete and detailed record of all German naval developments during the four years preceding the war.

Credit for this remarkable achievement must be awarded to the high officials of the ID who selected our secret service agents for duty in central Europe. The latter were few, very few, in number, but each was a specialist at his work, though none had actually served in the naval profession. They had taken up the task unwillingly, and only in response to an appeal to their patriotism. Needless to say, it entailed constant and serious personal risk. In the pursuit of his avocation the secret agent hazarded his liberty, and not seldom his life. Day and night he lived under a nerve strain that never relaxed.

Here is the personal testimony of one of these agents:

> *The work itself was thankless, perilous, and distinctly unremunerative, and those engaged in it too often found themselves caught in a web of intrigue and misunderstanding that has outlasted the war, and from which some may never hope to escape. It is safe to say that none of the survivors would ever dream of taking up intelligence work again, under any consideration whatsoever. The romantic associations of secret service exist largely in the imagination of writers who have had no experience of the real thing.*

> *For reasons that to me are inexplicable, intelligence work, how-*
> *ever hazardous it might be, and however valuable the results, was*
> *never sufficiently recognised by our home authorities as deserving*
> *of reward. It may be that this pointed neglect is due to an inher-*
> *ent prejudice against the whole business of espionage. If that be*
> *the attitude of the authorities, it is both illogical and unfair, in*
> *view of the fact, already stated, that every British member of the*
> *intelligence service abroad with whom I was acquainted took up*
> *the work, not in the hope of pecuniary reward, but from motives*
> *of patriotism, and in most cases only after repeated and urgent*
> *appeals by the ID chiefs in London.*

These are the words of a former agent of the naval secret service who, while harbouring no personal grievance, was indignant at the studied official neglect of colleagues who had abandoned promising careers at the dictates of patriotism.

Of recent years a number of books have appeared in which intelligence work is held up to derision.

Several of the authors are literary men who for some obscure reason were appointed to the secret service during the war. The original intention, no doubt, was to make use of their abilities for propaganda purposes, but under the topsy-turvy conditions then prevailing they eventually found themselves engaged in pseudo-intelligence work, principally in the Near East. As the proceedings in which they took part were futile and often far-cical, it is not surprising that they should have formed a low opinion of all secret service activities and caricatured them in their subsequent writings.

Thus, Mr Compton Mackenzie, in his *First Athenian Memories*, casts doubt on the value of any intelligence work except that conducted by an army in the field. But as Mr Mackenzie's experiences, so far as he has recorded them, were confined to Greece – where the conflicting policies of the Allied powers, coupled with the ill-controlled activities of their secret agents, brought about a situation that was at once Gilbertian and tragic – his sweeping condemnation of all secret service is based on inadequate knowledge.

Mr Mackenzie, in common with several other authors, obviously knows little of what this service accomplished by less theatrical methods before and during the war.

Sir Basil Thomson, in his book *The Allied Secret Service in Greece*, is also contemptuous of the secret agent and his work. True, he is magnanimous enough to admit that 'intelligence officers are as necessary to governments as they are to banks and business houses, and as long as they are under efficient and wise control they are no more dangerous to a state than a daily newspaper is dangerous to a household.'

But Sir Basil, like Mr Mackenzie, though with less excuse, is particularising on the *opera bouffe* antics of certain so-called intelligence agents in Greece, in which country the wartime atmosphere seems to have had a devastating effect on the mental balance and judgement of rulers, statesmen, diplomats, and lesser functionaries, irrespective of nationality.

Whatever the blunders and futilities of its political counterpart may have been, there is no doubt that the British naval intelligence service played an indispensable part in the winning of the war. Not only was it a prime factor in the defeat of the U-boat campaign, but by penetrating Germany's naval secrets before and after the outbreak of war it guaranteed us against surprises, which, if unsuspected, might have been sprung upon us with disastrous results. We can assert without fear of contradiction that had the admiralty acted without delay on the information supplied by British agents in central Europe from 1910 onward, we should have achieved a greater measure of success in the war at sea, and especially at the Battle of Jutland. This point will be elaborated in due course.

Throughout the pre-war period now under review our intelligence work abroad was handicapped by shortage of funds. Had more money been available it is certain that better results would have been attained. The marvel is that so much was done with such exiguous means.

In very exceptional circumstances our agents would, no doubt, have received adequate financial hacking, but in the course of their routine work they were expected to keep within the narrowest limits of expenditure. It follows, therefore, that bribery was but rarely resorted to as a means of procuring information. Nearly every valuable item of news had to be excavated by personal effort and at personal risk.

Thanks to the technical knowledge possessed by our agents, in striking contrast to those employed by Germany, they seldom wasted time, and never money, in pursuing a false trail. It is difficult for anyone who is conversant with the work done by these men between the autumn of 1910 and August 1914, to read with patience the burlesque accounts of 'intelligence' operations recently given to the world by more than one distinguished writer.

Here, in brief, are some of the results we owed to the unremitting vigilance, enterprise, skill, and courage of our secret service naval agents, who worked silently and patiently during those critical pre-war years.

The gist of the epoch-making German fleet Law Amendment Act of 1912, which foreshadowed a huge increase in the combative strength of the High Seas Fleet, was communicated to Whitehall weeks before the bill itself was tabled in the Reichstag.

The admiralty was supplied with ample information about:

- The German mobilisation plans;

- The emergency war measures that were to take effect as soon as the '*Mobilmachung*' signal was flashed to Kiel and Wilhelmshaven;

- The war stations of the High Seas Fleet and the special arrangements made for passing heavy ships through the Kiel Canal in a much shorter time than we had been led to believe was possible;

- The distribution of light squadrons, destroyers and submarines immediately after the declaration of war;

- The plans for reinforcing minesweeping flotillas and coastal patrols, afloat and ashore;

- The worldwide network of intelligence and coaling facilities that German consuls and other agents abroad had established in anticipation of operations by German commerce raiders.

Readers of Lord Jellicoe's volume, *The Grand Fleet*, will recall many passages that suggest we were utterly surprised by the abnormal powers of resistance displayed by German battle-ships and cruisers at Jutland and in earlier encounters, and not less by the high quality of their gunnery, ammunition, optical instruments, torpedoes, mines, and other equipment. Yet the archives of the naval intelligence division must contain documentary evidence to prove that all these German 'secrets' had been uncovered and reported by British agents long before the war.

The massive armour and extensive underwater protection of the German dreadnoughts were well known to the British Admiralty, which had received particulars and diagrams of practically every ship that Admiral Scheer commanded at Jutland. These had been secured by our agents years beforehand, and it was not their fault if the admiralty had neglected to produce armour-piercing shells capable of piercing the sides and decks of the German ships and detonating with full force inside.

An accurate description of the shell that the Germans used with deadly effect at Jutland was in the hands of the admiralty as far back as 1911, together with an account of its performance against armoured targets on the Krupp proving-ground at Meppen and specially constructed target ships at sea.

At or about the same date, drawings and details were furnished of the latest torpedoes in production at the government factory of Friedrichsort, near Kiel – these being the weapons by which the U-boats were destined to sink millions of tonnes of shipping.

All essential particulars of the German naval mine, which, though simple, was extraordinarily reliable and destructive, were contained in our pre-war ID files, yet in spite of this information we ourselves clung to an obsolete and inefficient type of mine for nearly two years after the outbreak of war.

Almost the only vital secret our agents failed to unearth was the manner in which the German Navy would be employed in a war with Great Britain. It is just as well that this remained hidden from us, for had it been otherwise we should have been completely deceived.

To elucidate this seeming paradox it is necessary to recall the singular state of affairs that existed in the German naval administration in August 1914.

Grand Admiral von Tirpitz had then served seventeen years as Secretary of State for the Navy. The High Seas Fleet was virtually his own creation. It had been built and organised in strict conformity with his own strategical theories, and, as we know from his own writing, he never doubted for a moment that when '*Der Tag*' dawned his imperial master would order him to forsake his desk in the Navy Office for the bridge of the flagship *Friedrich der Grosse* as Commander-in-Chief of the entire fleet.

All his plans were based upon that assumption. It was to be the apotheosis of those long years of single-minded and devoted service to the fatherland. And when the opportunity came he was determined to make the most of it. Not for him the timid, cautious strategy of keeping the fleet intact behind the shoals, minefields, and batteries of 'the wet triangle', preserving it as an asset for securing favourable peace terms. To him it was as a mighty sword for the striking of deadly blows at British sea power, which he had always recognised as the most formidable obstacle to the realisation of Germany's soaring ambitions.

Tirpitz, therefore, intended to seek a decisive battle with the British fleet at the earliest possible moment. He had a well-founded faith in the weapon he had forged, tempered and tested repeatedly in manoeuvres. If he exaggerated the power of the surface torpedo boat and under-estimated that of the submarine, he erred in the company of nearly all the senior naval officers of his day. The soundness of his policy in regard to capital ship construction and armament was brilliantly vindicated at Jutland. The German battlecruisers, especially, were magnificent fighting machines. That he was not personally responsible for the inadequate armament of the German light cruisers is conclusively proved by his memoirs.

But the declaration of hostilities brought him the bitterest disappointment of his life.

The Kaiser ignored his urgent request to be granted a free hand in directing the operations of the fleet, and retained in the chief command Admiral von Ingenohl, an officer of mediocre abilities who owed his advancement to the personal friendship of the Supreme War Lord and to prolonged service in the imperial yacht.

Nor was this all.

King Edward, many years before, had enraged his nephew by referring to the German fleet as 'Willie's toy'. This jest contained a profound truth. It soon became evident that Wilhelm II regarded the fleet as his personal property, to be cherished and conserved at all costs. The prospect of exposing his precious ships to the rude blasts of war filled him with dismay. He could view with equanimity the sacrifice of whole army corps on the battlefield, but he shrank from risking a single one of the dreadnoughts, which were, to him, majestic symbols of the aggrandisement and prestige of the Hohenzollern dynasty.

Therefore, immediately after Great Britain had declared war, he drafted with his own hand the notorious '*Operations-Befehl*', which doomed the German fleet to inactivity at the very moment when a prompt and resolute offensive might well have yielded the most fruitful results.

There is no question that even a partial German success in the North Sea would have delayed indefinitely the passage of the British Expeditionary Force to France, and vitally affected the whole war situation to the detriment of the Allied cause. Without the presence of the BEF, the Battle of the Marne might never have been fought, or, if it had been fought, the result would probably have been very different. Even a mass attack by German submarines in the southern area of the North Sea would have seriously embarrassed and retarded our military dispositions. Moreover, a bold offensive by the navy would have evoked intense enthusiasm in Germany and, by enhancing the popularity and prestige of what was, after all, a new and untried arm, might have so raised the morale of the sea service as to render impossible the humiliating events of November 1918.

But the Kaiser thought of none of these things. 'My ships must not be risked' was the purport of his 'operational orders'.

These forbade the High Seas Fleet to leave its sheltered anchorages except in the remote contingency of a British attack on the German coast. No ships of any importance were permitted to move without the express sanction of the Supreme War Lord, who arrogated to himself full executive control of the fleet. Thus, save for an abortive reconnaissance by a submarine flotilla and the despatch of a single minelayer towards the Thames Estuary, the entire German fleet lay idle at its moorings during the first crucial weeks of the war.

In vain did von Tirpitz plead for the *Entscheidungs-Schlacht*, the decisive battle, which at the very outset might have impeached Great Britain's command of the home seas and thus altered the subsequent course of the war.

The Kaiser's obstinate timidity where his ships were concerned found support from the Chancellor, Bethmann-Hollweg – who wanted the fleet to be kept as a bargaining asset at the peace table – and also from admirals who were jealous of von Tirpitz. Even before the war he had had contend with the enmity and intrigues of high officers who resented his unique position in the councils of the state. Between him and the chief of the *Marinekabinett* there existed a bitter feud, and as the department in question was empowered to make all naval appointments, subject only to the Kaiser's approval, it followed that von Tirpitz's recommendations were usually ignored and his protégés left out in the cold. Nor were his relations with the naval staff by any means cordial. Consequently, despite his virtual dictatorship of naval policy in regard to shipbuilding and equipment, he exercised only a very limited control over questions of personnel or strategy.

In this lack of coordination among the heads of the naval high command, coupled with the Kaiser's morbid dread of losing ships, we find the clue to the otherwise inexplicable management of German naval affairs during the first eighteen months of the war.

While the dissensions prevailing at the Berlin Navy Office were known to our secret service agents, they could not possibly forecast the effect on the operations of the German fleet in time of war.

The British Admiralty wisely prepared for all eventualities, including an immediate offensive by the High Seas Fleet, this latter being regarded as most probable. When, therefore, the long-expected conflict did eventuate, the absolute quiescence and the lack of initiative displayed by the German naval command caused much perplexity at Whitehall.

The first fruits of our intelligence work in Germany were

garnered almost at once. Thanks to our foreknowledge of the arrangements made, not only for despatching armed liners from Germany to attack the trade routes, but also for arming and equipping for the same purpose a large number of selected German merchantmen at sea or in neutral ports on the outbreak of war, we were able to take prompt counter-measures that had the effect of nipping these plans in the bud. The fact that only one armed liner (*Kaiser Wilhelm der Grosse*) left Germany in the first month of hostilities, instead of the fleet of such ships that had been earmarked for the purpose, was due in large part to the swift action taken by the British Admiralty 'from information received'.

This one among many concrete examples of the benefit we derived from our pre-war intelligence system in central Europe. Compared with the huge organisation built up subsequently, and presided over with conspicuous ability by Admiral Sir Reginald Hall, it was almost insignificant in personnel and resources. Yet its labours were singularly fruitful, as this book will show. That their full value has never been appreciated is no doubt due to the secrecy in which they were necessarily shrouded. But to those who knew the perils and anxieties of the service it is discouraging to find genuine intelligence work bracketed and pilloried with the comic-opera performances of amateur 'secret service' agents in neutral capitals during the war. It would be just as rational to introduce the pantomime policeman as a typical member of the Metropolitan Force.

CHAPTER 4

'SELLING THE DUMMY'

ONE OF THE by-products of the intense activity in naval intelligence work all over Europe during the years between 1911 and 1914 was the planting of 'faked' news in the way of known agents.

This was an entirely different thing, of course, from the attempts on the part of the purely mercenary spy bureaux to dispose of 'information' to any gullible customer. Any number of amusing stories can be told of that aspect of the work.

For example, very shortly after the war began a plausible individual wormed his way into the confidence of a prominent British naval authority and offered him (for a price) plans of the latest German submarines.

He produced a printed folding diagram, large enough to occupy a complete spread of a daily newspaper, and closely annotated in German.

The authority was rather impressed. It looked like a real find.

Fortunately he had at hand a colleague who knew Germany well. This man was called into consultation. And he pointed out, with as much gravity as he could muster, that the plan was a print produced by a well-known Berlin publisher as an extra illustration to a boys' magazine, and that it had been sold on the bookstalls in thousands, at a shilling a time, for months before the war. It contained no information of any sort about German submarine construction that could not be found in the most elementary textbooks!

That same plausible gentleman, however, scored a minor triumph when he sold to the editor of a certain English review a ridiculous article on the German naval defences. The editor was unlucky. He had no colleague with first-hand German knowledge whom he could consult, and the article duly appeared, to the intense amusement of all those who knew the facts.

An attempt to 'sell the dummy', which may have been inspired from German sources or may have been a commercial effort on the part of a spy, led to very careful investigation of the admiralty a year or two before the war.

The would-be vendor, a German, offered a large-scale map of Borkum, which we regarded as the key of the German coastal defences in the Bight, and about which, as everyone knew, we had a quite legitimate curiosity. It was an enormous map, and it bore the imprint of the naval hydrographic bureau in Berlin.

It showed in full detail the batteries and other defensive works on the island, and at first sight was decidedly impressive. The German asked a very big price for it, something far beyond the means of our intelligence service to pay for out of its normal budget. But the offer was too promising to reject out of hand.

In order to present the case for it as strongly as possible in the right quarter, the head of the department decided to check it up with the information our own men had obtained about Borkum. And he found that the map was wrong in every important point!

The probability is that the attempt to plant it with us was officially inspired in Berlin. When the German called for his money he was politely shown the door but the map was retained by us as a souvenir, and thereafter adorned one of the walls at ID headquarters.

Lord Fisher always claimed to have achieved the outstanding success of 'selling the dummy' when he caused bogus plans of our first battlecruisers to be passed through to Berlin, as narrated in a previous chapter.

Lord Fisher made the story public in his memoirs, and since then it has been categorically repudiated by more than one German authority, notably Dr Bürkner, but there is nothing inherently improbable in the Fisher version, and the very fact that the Germans built the *Blücher* after we had laid down the first battlecruisers indicates strongly that they did not suspect the real nature of the 'armoured cruisers' included in the British programme for 1905.

Nevertheless, towards the end of 1908 it became privately known in British shipbuilding circles that plans, generally believed to be a complete set, of our first battlecruisers had vanished in transit between a shipyard and the admiralty. The boxes that should have contained them were intact and sealed, but from each box some of the plans were missing, and, collectively, the missing parts provided a definite guide to the design of the ships.

The first German battlecruiser, the *Von der Tann*, was laid down in 1909.

We know that the German intelligence department did

purchase a considerable number of 'dummies'. For some psychological reason the Russians were uncommonly good at planting spurious documents with the intelligence departments of other powers. The German Admiralty was as much interested in the Russian coastline and the fortifications of Riga, Libau and Reval as we were in the Heligoland Bight defences. It will be remembered that the German Baltic forces launched several attacks in the Moon Sound area of the Baltic during the war, and that on the first two occasions their efforts were remarkably unsuccessful.

One reason for this was that before the war the Russian counter-espionage bureau had planted with the German Admiralty (for a very large sum of money) wholly misleading plans of the defences in that area. British intelligence men who were in close touch with the Russians in the early months of the war were assured that the Germans had paid hundreds of thousands of marks for the plans, which were very skilfully prepared and full of the most detailed information – all of it wrong.

British intelligence agents working in Germany were either more shrewd or more fortunate than their opponents. Numberless efforts were made to palm off spurious plans on them, but rarely, very rarely, with success. At the admiralty it was well understood that material that came from our agents had been thoroughly sifted before being sent home, and that consequently there was good reason to credit it.

Our agents abroad dodged most of the spurious material, partly because they were so very careful about the men with whom they dealt. As will be made clear in the course of this volume, most of them depended for their facts almost entirely on personal observation. This in itself would have prevented them from falling into the traps laid for them. They were well aware of the danger of negotiating with any stranger who offered to furnish secret information. *Agents provocateurs* were ubiquitous and unwearying in their efforts to lay snares for our men. For that reason the latter refused time and again even to look at material that was offered to them, on the very simple plea that as they were not interested in naval or military secrets there was no point in inspecting the plans or other documents that the obliging *agent provocateur* might propose to show them.

Even so, a good deal of spurious matter did come their way. Early in 1912 one of their number was offered by a man, whom he knew to be trustworthy, diagrams revealing the secrets of the latest German dreadnoughts, the *Nassau*, *Helgoland* and *Kaiser* classes. In view of the source from which they were proffered, our agent felt justified in examining the plans; but as he had already placed with the home intelligence department complete details of all the ships in question, he did not expect to be able to do much more than verify his own report by the new material.

When the plans were laid before him it did not take five minutes for him to discover that they were spurious. What is more, he realised that he himself was probably in a position of grave danger. The sequel is best told in his own words:

The man I got them from had never tricked me before, but here, as plain as a pikestaff, was a set of faked plans. So far as I could see, there could only be one reason for their existence. The German counter-espionage had laid a trap for me.

For about half an hour I really knew what fear was.

I got those diagrams out of my possession in a few minutes, but even then I could not be sure that I had not left finger-prints on them that might be fatal to me.

I was in my own rooms, and every sound in the house made me quake. I expected to see the door open any moment and a couple of security police come in.

And, looking back on the incident, I see how inevitably a man in a panic does the foolish thing. I know that I did, and yet at the time it seemed to be the only possible course.

Slipping round the post office, I sent a telegram to myself, calling me to England to see my family.

In a cold sweat, I sat in a café for half an hour or so, to allow time for the telegram to reach my rooms and for my landlady to take it in. I wanted my alibi to be as complete as possible. And all the time I overlooked the very obvious point that the place of origin of the telegram was not London, but the German town I was living in! Months afterwards, when I was talking to 'C' about the adventure, he showed me the folly of this move.

Eventually I strolled back to my rooms, outwardly as calm and normal as usual, and was handed the telegram. Having told my landlady the message it contained, I went out to buy railway tickets and reserve a sleeper.

There were several hours to wait before the train was due.

Only those who have expected to be arrested at any moment can realise what I went through during that time. As far as possible I had to keep to my ordinary routine, in case I was being watched. The fact that I had got rid of the diagrams relieved my mind to some extent, though I was uncomfortably aware that the chance of doing so might only have occurred because the security police had blundered as to the time at which they were to visit my rooms and make the capture.

During those few hours, my imagination ran riot. As I walked along the platform to my coach on the train I expected every instant to feel a hand on my shoulder. It did not seem possible that I could get clear away. I went into the sleeper, and shut myself in, though what good that could do I cannot imagine, since the names of all those occupying coupés are on the list in the possession of the conductor.

The train started, and so far nothing had happened.

But that did not end my ordeal. We had several hours of travel through German territory before we reached the frontier, and there were a number of stopping places. Assuming the raid on my rooms to have been planned for after dark, there was still plenty of time for telegraphic instructions to hold me up.

As we approached the frontier I lay on my berth, fully dressed, in an agony of apprehension. I confess quite frankly that my nerve had temporarily gone. After living for several years in daily peril of detection, this collapse was not, perhaps, surprising.

At the frontier station we stopped as usual. I had given my passport to the conductor for him to show in order that I should not be disturbed, and there I lay in the darkness and the silence – waiting. Most of us associate railway stations with noise, but a frontier post in the small hours is silent as the grave, except for the occasional sound of the shunter's horn or the footsteps of some official along the platform.

I could hear my heart beating, so profound was the silence in that coupé. My breath was coming in gasps. Frankly, I was just about at the end of my strength.

All at once the train began to move. It gathered speed.

I sat up. And the next minute was violently sick.

It isn't romantic, but that's how things are in real life. And once we were across the frontier, I got a grip on myself. I saw what an utter fool I had been to clear out so abruptly.

It wouldn't do to go back at once, however. So I stopped off in

Brussels, called on some friends, and stayed a day or two with them. Then, fully master of my nerves once more, I went boldly back to my old headquarters in Germany and resumed my work, both pretended and real.

I had been the victim of a false alarm. As I found out afterwards, my man had got hold of some spurious diagrams from somewhere, but they had not been deliberately planted on him, and to this day I don't believe the German security service ever had the slightest idea of what my real mission was during the years I worked under their noses.

Another man who was present when this story was told had also worked for our intelligence service in Germany.

'I once had a bad fright,' he said, 'but mine went a bit further than yours. I was actually detained on suspicion – and then got away with it.'

He paused, and his listeners sat in expectant silence.

'It does turn your stomach over, doesn't it?' he added after a moment, and then went on:

I had been up in one of the German naval bases, with a perfectly legitimate business to cloak me, and had gathered quite a lot of good information. I naturally did not send in a report from there, but waited till I was in an inland city. Then I wrote out a pretty full despatch in code, and put it into an envelope, with the address typewritten. I wrote another letter, just a chatty note, to a friend in Leeds, addressed the envelope in my own handwriting, choosing an envelope of a different shape and colour from that containing the report, and went out to post them both.

I had just dropped them into the pillar-box when I felt a touch on my arm. A German policeman and a man in plain clothes were standing by me.

'Are you Herr So-and-so?' asked the man in plain clothes.

I admitted it.

'Would you mind coming with us to the town hall to show your papers?'

It was a most polite way of putting the request, and anyway I couldn't refuse. So I accompanied them in a cab, though I did not enjoy the ride. It really looked as if the game was up.

At the town hall I was taken into a room, there to be confronted by the local chief of police and a man whom I at once spotted as one of the senior men in the German naval intelligence department. That made it pretty certain that my number was up.

'Did you post some letters just now?' I was asked, after they had established my identity and examined my papers thoroughly.

I admitted having posted one letter, told them quite frankly what the envelope looked like, and the name and address it bore, and gave them an outline of the contents – all the gossip I had sent to my friend at Leeds.

Then they brought in a mail-bag. All the letters in that box had been collected immediately after I had posted mine, and had been sent round to the town hall in this sealed bag. The seals were broken and the letters turned out on a table. Of course, the only one for which I had any eyes was that containing my report. It seemed to me by far the most conspicuous letter in the heap.

The Chief of Police went through the collection slowly and methodically until he came to the letter of which I had told them.

'You permit me?' he asked with ironic politeness, picking up a paper knife to slit open the envelope.

With perfect calm, and equal irony (I hope), I bowed my consent.

He opened the letter, and he and the intelligence officer read it through. The contents, of course, were exactly as I had described them.

And all the time that other infernal letter lay neglected on the table, and I had all I could do not to stare at it. The incident was really funny, though I am afraid the joke did not strike me just then.

They scrutinised my Leeds letter with a magnifying glass. They tested it for secret inks. They tried to read a cipher into it, and that part of the performance I really did enjoy. The Berlin intelligence man had brought several code books with him, and he tried them all on that perfectly innocent letter.

Of course, they went through the pile for another envelope like mine, or for one bearing similar handwriting. They had my secret report in their hands half a dozen times at least, but it aroused no suspicion, though the first time they picked it up my heart did miss a beat.

At length, near midnight, they released me, with apologies and an unconvincing explanation that they were on the track of an international crook of whose appearance they had been advised by New York and Scotland Yard, and that I unfortunately bore some resemblance to him. The end of the interview was really a very pretty little comedy, both sides lying hard, they about their imaginary crook, and I about my belief in their explanations. Then I went back to my hotel, to rout out the night porter and order a double brandy and soda-dringend.

The most amusing feature of the story is that I stayed on in Germany doing ID work for another couple of years and, so far as I know, from that time onward I was never even shadowed.

In connection with the traffic in confidential ship plans a singular comedy occurred in Brussels in 1913.

A shipwright employed at the Blohm and Voss yard in Hamburg absconded with a set of blue prints detailing the internal arrangements and armour disposition of the battlecruiser *Seydlitz*, which was then building at the yard.

They were absolutely genuine, and the renegade shipwright, having heard about the international spy bureau in Brussels, went there to try to sell his stolen wares.

The simple audacity of the man was too much for the 'experts' who traded in military secrets. They simply did not believe him. They assumed him be as tricky as themselves, and flatly refused to do business.

He had gone to Brussels with visions of a fortune. But after a few days his funds ran out. He actually touted the blueprints round some of the low cafés of the Belgian capital, trying to raise £5 on them, but did not find anyone who would believe his story.

Eventually, he managed to scrape a little money together, and with this made his way back to Germany, still carrying the blueprints with him.

He escaped detection at the time, and the story would never have become known but for a queer trick of fate years later – after the war, in fact. Then his crime was discovered, he was tried for treason, and sentence to twelve years' imprisonment.

The story throws a queer sidelight on the mentality of those who dealt in naval and military secrets as commodities to be sold to the highest bidder. They themselves dealt in so much spurious material that they invariably suspected anything that was offered to them. The men engaged in that trade were, of course, fundamentally dishonest. They were the rabble of the espionage world, and most of them made a living not by procuring information, but by betraying others to the security police of any country that would pay their fees. The majority were known by sight to the regular intelligence men, who carefully steered clear of them, and had the unfortunate Captain Bertrand Stewart, whose story is told elsewhere, been in touch with the ID headquarters, he would probably never have fallen into the trap set for him by the man Rue.

CHAPTER 5

'THE SONG OF THE SWORD'
– AND HOWITZERS

W HEN THE GERMAN legions swarmed over the Belgian frontier in the early days of August 1914, public opinion in the Allied countries was encouraged to believe that the tidal wave of invasion would be stemmed by the 'impregnable' fortresses of Liège and Namur. The massive steel and concrete ramparts of the Belgian citadels were supposed to be proof against the heaviest artillery, and so, no doubt, they were against the most powerful mobile guns of which the world at large had cognisance.

But Germany had up her sleeve a trump card in the shape of the gigantic 16.5-inch howitzers, the 'Fat Berthas', whose levinbolts soon reduced the forts of Liège to a heap of pulverised ruins. So far as the general public was concerned, the appearance of these mammoth cannon was one of the most dramatic surprises of the war, but to the staffs of the Allied armies it was no surprise at all.

Nearly twelve months before the outbreak of war the existence of these howitzers was discovered by an agent of the British naval secret service, and duly reported by him to headquarters in London.

Presumably, therefore, the information was transmitted to Paris and Brussels, for it was obvious that the 'Berthas' had been built for no other purpose than the battering down of the frontier defences of Germany's neighbours.

How such a portentous but purely military secret came to be penetrated by a naval agent is a curious story, now told for the first time.

A few prefatory remarks may be offered about the 'Fat Berthas' and other heavy artillery that the German general staff, as they fondly believed, had prepared unknown to the outer world. As far back as 1900, espionage reports on the newly constructed fortresses of Liège and Namur in Belgium, and of Verdun, Toul, and Belfort in France, in the building of which ferro-concrete and stout armour plating had been largely used, led the German general staff to overhaul its siege artillery. As the heaviest gun then available was the 8.2-inch howitzer, which was considered to be ineffective against the new defences, an order was placed with Krupps for several batteries of 12-inch 'mortars' (to employ the official designation, i.e. '*Mörser*'), the existence of which was kept a close secret. Ten years later, when the German staff had fully made up its mind to adopt the Schlieffen plan of invading France via Belgium, and it therefore became necessary to ensure the speedy reduction of Liège and Namur, lest, by holding up the German hosts, they should cause the whole scheme to go awry,

Krupps were invited to submit specifications for the heaviest howitzers it was feasible to transport by road.

Designs prepared by Professor Rausenberger, of Krupps' ordnance staff, for a 16.5-inch (42-cm) howitzer were approved, and production began forthwith. In 1912 four of these monster guns were completed. They were housed in a building at Essen that was guarded day and night, and, save by the men who had built them and the crews selected to work them, their existence remained practically unknown outside the Ministry of War in Berlin.

They were indeed formidable engines of destruction, hurling an armour-piercing explosive shell of 1,980 lb at a range of nearly 7 miles. Descending from the blue at a steep angle, these thunderbolts crashed irresistibly through the thickest, concrete, bomb proofs and the toughest armour plate.

Each howitzer was moved to the scene of action by four tractors, hitched to trucks containing, respectively, the gun itself, the carriage, an assembly crane, and the crew. The terrible effects of their fire on the forts at Liège has been vividly described by eyewitnesses. But with the reduction of the Belgian strongholds their usefulness was at an end. In November 1914, they arrived on the Western Front, where they were soon found to be of no value against the entrenched positions that were the only targets in view. A few months later they were withdrawn.

So much for the 'Fat Berthas' themselves. To this day, as we have said, it is widely believed that they took the Allies completely by surprise, whereas, in truth, their existence was discovered nearly a year before the war, and fairly complete details of them were given in an intelligence report transmitted to London in the autumn of 1913.

From the practical point of view, no doubt, the information was not of much use. The British War Office had long known of the German plan to strike at France through Belgium, though the French authorities continued to turn a blind eye to the most positive evidence on this point. Belgium, even if apprised of the new German howitzers, would have had no time to reinforce the defences of Liège on the necessary scale. So there was nothing to be done but await the blow, which duly fell.

Nevertheless, the story of the discovery of this secret deserves inclusion because of the singular and dramatic features it presents.

In the late summer of 1913 an agent of our naval secret service, whom we will call Brown, was in Hanover, where he had several German acquaintances. He had, of course, perfectly good reasons for his visit to that city, since a legitimate occupation (which served as a 'cover' not only for his residence in Germany, but also for the almost constant travelling that his real work entailed) was as essential to the intelligence agent as the pursuit of cricket was to 'Raffles'. Amongst Brown's friends in Hanover was an army reserve officer, who was inordinately proud of the privilege of wearing the Kaiser's uniform on certain occasions. By the Prussian regular soldier these reservist officers were slightingly labelled as 'civilians with extenuating circumstances', but they were none the less keen and efficient soldiers who largely formed the backbone of Germany's second-line formations during the Great War.

That night Brown's friend, Herr Schultz, was attending a reserve officers' reunion dinner, more properly termed a *Bier-Abend*, and he was kind enough to invite Brown to accompany him as his guest, these occasions being very informal and *gemütlich*. Brown accepted with alacrity, knowing by experience how expansive and communicative the sternest Prussian often became under the mellowing influence of plentiful beer.

Good fellowship and camaraderie were the order of the evening. Among the other guests were eight or nine regular officers of the Hanover garrison who were relatives or close friends of their hosts.

The simple meal over, beer mugs were refilled, cigars were lighted, and the company 'proceeded to harmony.' Old favourites, such as the '*Gaudeamus*', 'Was Martin Luther *spricht*' and '*Wer niemals einen Rausch gehabt, der ist kein braver Mann*', were succeeded by the more classical melodies of Schubert and Schumann, rendered by accomplished singers who are invariably to be found in any German gathering, irrespective of class or profession. After these came tuneful *Volkslieder*, and the stirring patriotic ballads of which German music has so rich a store. The latter harmonised well with the atmosphere of the evening. Round the long, bare table sat uniformed officers of all ranks, from a grizzled colonel of artillery to a pink-cheeked Sapper subaltern whose first tunic had but lately left its tissue-paper wrappings.

In physiognomy and mannerism the company was a microcosm of the Germanic race. One saw the high cheek-bones and snub features of the East Prussian, in whose veins – deny it as indignantly as he would – runs Tartar blood; the blond, blue-eyed, athletic Rhinelander, who has only to pass through the hands of a Savile-Row tailor to become, to all outward appearance, a typical well-bred Englishman; the short, dark, vivacious Saxon, whose naturally easygoing temperament peeps through the veneer of restraint and discipline imposed by a military training that is Prussian to the core, despite the nominal independence of the Saxon kingdom; the jovial, loud-voiced, but choleric Bavarian, whose somewhat unruly instincts, checked and tempered by the same Prussian discipline, make him one of the doughtiest fighting men in Europe.

These Teutonic warriors are taking their ease, with belts unbuckled and stiff collars loosened. On side tables are piled their red-lined cloaks, high-crowned caps and gleaming swords. Old comrades pledge one another in deep draughts of *Pilsner* or *Münchner*, beverages exhilarating but not too potent. Jests crackle to and fro across the board, and now and then an explosion of laughter follows some Rabelaisian anecdote by the genial captain of the crack *Maikäfer* Regiment, who is the best raconteur of the evening.

A lull in the conversation, and then the strains of 'The Song of the Sword' with its almost mystical, staccato verses, which the Saxon poet Körner penned only a few hours before he fell at the Battle of the Nations at Leipzig in 1813, steal through the room.

A murmur of astonishment runs round the table, for the singer is the English guest, yet he is singing this essentially German martial song with all the impassioned fervour of one of Körner's own countrymen:

> Du Schwert an meiner Linken,
> Was soll dein heitres Blinken?
> Schaust mich so freundlich an,
> Hab' meine Freud daran,
> Hurra! Hurra! Hurra!
> O, seliges Umfangen,
> Ich harre mit Verlangen.

Du, Bräutgam, hole mich,
Mein Kränzchen bleibt für Dich.
Hurra! Hurra! Hurra!

The song is greeted with rapturous applause, which is, perhaps, less of a tribute to the quality of the rendering than to the singer himself for entering so heartily into the spirit of the thing.

Wunderbar! Ausgezeichnet! Dass ist ja etwas eigenartig, nicht wahr? *An Englishman singing our* Vaterland's Lieder. Bitte, lieber Kamerad, singen Sie doch weiter. Kennen Sie 'Die Wacht am Rhein', Der Gott Der Eisen wachsen liess, 'Deutschland über Alles', oder sowas?

To refuse would be a churlish return for the kindly, spontaneous hospitality of his hosts, so the guest obliges to the best of his ability. And his fervour is genuine enough, for music and poetry should know no frontiers, and these German war songs are among the best ever written:

Es braust ein Ruf wie Donnerhall,
Und hunderttausend Männerschall:
Zum Rhein, zum Rhein, zum deutschen Rhein,
Wer will des Strömes Hüter sein?
Lieb Vaterland, magst ruhig sein,
Fest steht und treu die Wacht,
Die Wacht am Rhein!

After this the singer was hailed as good comrade and brother. Polite enough before, his hosts now vied with each other in friendly demonstration. His health was drunk with acclamation, and he was not sorry when the enthusiasm died down and he was left in peace to listen to the general conversation.

It had turned, as was but natural, on the prospects of war, for in 1913 thunderclouds were already lowering on the political horizon of Europe. Ordinarily the presence of a stranger would have enjoined reticence, but the beer had circulated merrily, the atmosphere was convivial, and Mr Brown's vocal efforts had made him free of the fold.

That war was not only inevitable, but near at hand, was the unanimous opinion, openly expressed. There was much talk of King Edward's *Einkreisungs-Politik*, the 'encirclement of Germany' legend, which had been sedulously fostered by every means of publicity at the command of the government. But to these soldiers Great Britain was only a vague and contingent enemy. They saw in France the star villain of the piece, with Russia as her close confederate. They exhibited an unbridled hatred and contempt for *die Franzosen*, whom all agreed must be taught such a lesson as would purge them, once and for all, of their bellicose fever.

They despised the Russians, too, and it was noticeable that those of the company who hailed from the eastern marches of Prussia were foremost in breathing fire and thunder against the Tsarist Empire – probably because of their own partly Slav extraction.

But despite their martial ardour, one and all were alive to the dangers of a war on two fronts. Supremely confident of their ability to crush either France or Russia single-handed, they were less positive as to the issue if both powers had to be fought simultaneously. They attached little value to the military cooperation of their Austrian allies, and some of those present deplored the tendency of the German Foreign Office to give unquestioning support to the devious policy that Austria-Hungary was then, as always, pursuing in the Balkans – the European powder magazine that the fates had timed to explode only twelve months later.

'Of course we shall have to fight on both fronts,' declared an Infantry Major. 'The only question is, Where shall we mass our main strength and deal the heaviest blows? My view is that we ought to keep strictly on the defensive in the East and concentrate on a tremendous drive into France. We must smash right through them' – emphasising his point with a vigorous sweep of the arm – 'hammering our way to Paris, and beyond if necessary, until all the fight is beaten out of them. We should get to Paris in a month, at latest. Then we could send divisions back to the East in time to stop a serious breakthrough, for everybody knows that Russia cannot fully mobilise in less than six weeks.'

'All very well,' said another officer; 'but don't forget that we cannot burst into France until her frontier forts are in our hands. It is not a question of merely containing them while our main army marches past. They are so placed that we cannot deploy until their guns are silenced.'

The Major stared coolly at his colleague.

'What forts are those? Do you imagine that we are going to break our heads against Belfort, Toul, and Verdun? No, there's a better way than that, and everybody knows we are going to take it. Yes, everybody', he repeated, banging his fist on the table. 'For what else have we built those colossal railway stations at Eupen and Malmedy? It's an understood thing that we shall be over the Luxemburg and Belgian border almost from the word "go". There's no secret about it at all!'

'But that means a breach of neutrality,' objected one of his hearers:

> And suppose Belgium resisted? Her army may not amount to much, but we couldn't take Liège and Namur in our stride. They are said to be as strong as any of the French forts, and we should have to begin a regular siege. And what about Antwerp, which may prove a still tougher nut? But it would have to be cracked, unless we were content to leave it, with perhaps the whole Belgian army and some French divisions inside, as a perpetual menace to our right flank and line of communications?

The young engineer officer, hitherto shy and silent in the presence of so many seniors, now joined in:

> Liège is certainly very strong. I spent a month in Belgium last summer, and made as close an inspection as possible of Liège and Namur. The big-gun cupolas at Liège are said to be armoured with 9-inch plating, and the ferro-concrete shelters are given in our textbooks as 4 ft thick. If that be so, they could probably defy our 12-inch howitzers.

'Ah,' said the Major:

> We're not relying on those. My brother Ulrich, who's in the War Ministry, told me something the other day that would give our neighbours across the border a pretty shock. We've got something much heavier than the 12-inch, so much heavier as to be almost unbelievable. Ganz geheim, of course, but they're all ready at Essen. The shells are colossal; in fact, they weigh about ------.

The speaker did not finish his sentence, for the Colonel, who had been chatting with a friend, and only at that moment appeared to become aware of the conversation further down the table, suddenly rapped with his knuckles on the board and exclaimed '*Achtung!*'

There was an embarrassed silence, and the garrulous Major slowly reddened beneath his tan. Then the Colonel rose, and beckoned to the Major, who, with a muttered '*Zu Befehl, Herr Oberst*', joined him in a corner of the room. It was very obvious that the gallant infantryman was receiving a lecture for having talked 'shop' rather too freely.

'*Ach, Quatsch*,' exclaimed another officer in low tones. 'What's the old man fussing about? We're all friends here.'

He shot a glance at Mr Brown, who, apparently unaware of the slightly strained atmosphere, was discussing with his neighbour the respective merits of light and dark beer. The two officers soon returned to the table, but the Major was no longer in a talkative mood, and soon took his leave.

Two days later Mr Brown's business took him to Wiesbaden, or so he told his Hanoverian friends. But apparently he got into the wrong train, for that same evening found him at Düsseldorf, which attractive city lies within easy distance of Essen. It is unnecessary to go into his subsequent activities in any detail. He spent most of the time at Essen, returning to Düsseldorf every night and sending a number of business telegrams to Brussels – whence, strange to say, they were instantly relayed to London.

On the evening of the fifth day Brown was seated in a little *estaminet* at Roermond, a tiny Dutch hamlet within sight of the German frontier. A westbound train drew up at the station and several passengers descended, among them a man wearing the unmistakable ill-made but respectable Sunday garments of a German artisan. He glanced about him rather furtively, and remained on the platform until the rest of the passengers had dispersed. Then, having made inquiry of a porter, he set off towards the *estaminet* where Brown awaited him.

The two men took not the slightest notice of each other. Brown continued to read his paper and sip his beer, while at another table the German artisan stolidly munched sandwiches between copious draughts from the largest *Stein* the little inn could boast. Presently Brown paid his score and left, taking the long straight road that runs parallel with the railway until he reached a side path bordered with stunted poplars. He turned into this and followed it for a few hundred yards, then sat down and lighted his pipe. It was a radiant autumn afternoon. The flat Dutch landscape, over which the eye could range for miles, seemed deserted, but Brown, keeping well under cover of the poplars, waited patiently, his gaze fixed on the dusty highway whence he had come.

In twenty minutes he saw a figure approaching from the direction of Roermond. It came slowly on until it reached the poplar-bordered lane, halted there for a moment, then plodded down the lane. Brown rose to his feet as the man advanced.

The latter, in spite of his outward stolidity, was somewhat excited.

'I'm sure there was an Essen policeman on the train,' he said nervously. 'But he didn't get out at Roermond, so I suppose it's all right.'

'You certainly haven't been followed from there', Brown reassured him. 'I've been watching the road for the past half-hour, and no one has passed save yourself. Where are the papers?' he held out his hand.

'Not so fast, *mein Herr*,' said the other. 'How do I know you have got what you promised me?' Brown took from his wallet a fat roll of German banknotes and counted them before the man's eyes, which glistened at the sight. He in his turn opened his coat, produced a pocket knife, and ripped open the stitches in the lining, out of which he took several sheets of paper.

These he proffered to Brown, who took them, while still retaining the wad of banknotes.

'One moment,' he said, as the German, suspicious and growing angry, demanded the money. 'I must look through these first to make sure that you have delivered the goods. Sit down and smoke this excellent cigar. I shall not keep you many minutes.' Still grumbling, his companion complied, while Brown, having run swiftly through the papers, settled down to a more careful scrutiny.

'I do not see the blueprint you promised,' he remarked. The other hastily explained:

> It was impossible to obtain, mein Herr. Schmidt got cold feet at the last moment, and said he would have nothing to do with the business. I told him the Ehrhardt people at Düsseldorf only wanted the plans for business purposes, but I think he smelt a rat. He said that the typed descriptive notes didn't matter, because half a dozen of his colleagues might have supplied them; but if a blueprint were missed he would at once come under suspicion. But there is a rough drawing, which he told us gave all the important details.

Brown did not answer, but continued to study the papers. Finally he appeared to be satisfied, placed them in his pocket, and handed over the money without further parley. He watched amusedly as the German hurriedly sewed the notes into the lining of his coat with a needle and thread he had produced from a capacious purse.

'Your idea of a hiding place is rather primitive, my friend,' he said at length. 'If I were searching you I should begin by ripping opening your coat.'

The man was obviously taken aback.

'It's the best place I could think of,' he grumbled:

> *Anyway, in spite of seeing that policeman, I'm sure nobody suspects anything. Friedrich Muller is known at Essen as a respectable man who has been at the works for twenty years, and never had a black mark against him. Besides, what harm, after all, is there in handing over a few trade secrets to a rival firm at Düsseldorf? The big people might kick up a fuss if they knew, but it's not really a crime, if you look at it reasonably.*

Mr Brown listened to this rather clumsy attempt to allay the prickings of a conscience, which even the goodly plaster of banknotes had not wholly soothed.

'Quite so,' he observed drily. 'I have no doubt that Herr Friedrich Muller is a perfectly respectable member of society, though I have not had the pleasure of meeting him.'

His companion started violently and turned pale. 'But, *mein Herr*, I am Friedrich Muller, as you very well know.'

'Indeed,' said Brown, lighting a cigar; 'I rather fancied you were Otto Behncke, residing at 42 Brücke-Strasse, third étage. Come, come,' he continued, raising his hand as the other began to bluster a denial, 'I naturally took the trouble to check your identity when our little transaction was first broached. But, believe me, there's no harm done, and you have nothing to fear. You may have opportunities of earning much more money in future, with just as little risk, if you care to do so.'

Three days later Behncke's typescript and drawings were in the hands of the intelligence department in London, by whom, no doubt, they were promptly transmitted to the War Office. They gave a fairly complete description of the German 16.5-inch howitzers, mountings, and ammunition, and of the method of transporting them. There is reason to believe that the authenticity of the documents was doubted at first, though later they were passed as genuine, as indeed they were. But while Mr Brown's divergence from his purely naval intelligence duties in pursuit of an important but purely military secret had proved entirely successful, the official appreciation of his achievement was not warm enough to encourage him to step outside his own particular field again. Nor did his partiality for German *Volkslieder* produce any other noteworthy results in connection with his work, though it was undoubtedly valuable as a passport into circles where information was to be gleaned.

But more than once in the future was he to sing again the stirring words of '*Deutschland über Alles*', not as a soloist, but as one of a huge chorus. The first occasion was the launch of a great battlecruiser at Hamburg, shortly before the war. The second was at Bremen, in August 1928, when the venerable and justly revered President of the German Republic, Field-Marshal von Hindenburg, launched the giant Atlantic liner *Bremen*, in the presence of a vast concourse. So infectious was the enthusiasm roused by this event that Mr Brown was by no means the only Englishman there who joined heartily in the German national anthem that swelled to a mighty crescendo as the magnificent ship glided down the ways into the waters of the Elbe. A great ship is a work of art, as Ruskin truly said, and it will be a bad day for civilisation when appreciation of a masterpiece of art is influenced by national prejudice.

CHAPTER 6

HUE AND CRY!

ODERN WRITERS ON criminology have made us familiar with the methods of detection peculiar to Scotland Yard, the Paris Sûreté, and the Berlin Hauptpolizeamt, respectively. In German detective practice, we are told, the resources of science are invoked to a degree unknown in other countries. Be that as it may, the German police department, which in pre-war days was responsible for dealing with cases of espionage, had many more failures than triumphs. At no time, indeed, did it score an outstanding success.

For at least two years before the Great War the police were making prodigious efforts to locate and trap the principal foreign intelligence agents who were working in Germany, some of whom, in spite of the extreme circumspection with which they went about their task, had at length fallen under suspicion.

Their connection with the British secret service may not have been definitely known, but it was certainly suspected, for their correspondence began to be tampered with, and they often found themselves under surveillance. All this, of course, made their work more difficult, but, strange to say, did not seriously interrupt it. That foreigners resident in Germany, strongly suspected of being engaged in intelligence work, should have been able not only to continue their activities, but even to conceal their whereabouts from the German police for months at a time, may seem incredible, but it is none the less true.

One of these men remained in Germany for three and a half years, travelling the country from end to end, visiting every naval base and armament centre in the Reich, and gathering a mass of secret data on naval affairs; yet for the greater part of this period he eluded the utmost vigilance of the authorities, and on the few occasions when they did stumble upon his tracks they were unable to secure a vestige of concrete evidence against him. And all this happened in what was claimed to be the most highly organised state in the world!

Innumerable traps were laid for this elusive agent, but usually they were so obvious that only a simpleton would have walked into them. When the police found themselves impotent they enlisted the cooperation of the German Admiralty, and even of the press, but still did not succeed in laying hands on this much-wanted intruder. He came and went at will, attempted little or no disguise, had confidential transactions with German subjects who well knew his business, and, only a few weeks before the outbreak of war, departed quietly and unmolested from German territory.

During his forty-two months of intelligence work in the country he met and conversed with scores of naval officers, including Grand Admiral von Tirpitz himself; many police officials, including the redoubtable Herr von Jagow, president of the Berlin Police; naval architects, engineers, gunnery, armour plate and submarine experts.

He attended meetings of the German Navy League, and was on social terms with some of the protagonists of the big-navy campaign. He knew the inside of nearly every dockyard in the country, and could have described from memory the salient features of the coast defences from Emden to Sylt, and from Flensburg to the Russian border. And, to crown all, he was at one period a daily visitor at the police headquarters in a great German city, where a desk was placed at his disposal and official documents were laid before him for inspection! Although these exploits may sound fantastic, and more suggestive of Arsène Lupin than of a living individual, we have verified them by evidence that is unimpeachable.

During the latter part of his stay in Germany this agent evidently became an object of suspicion, for his correspondence was intercepted and opened (so clumsily as to betray the fact at a glance), he was often shadowed, and many attempts were made to implicate him in dubious transactions.

The methods employed were so inept as to excite derision. Take for example the system of shadowing. A detective would follow the suspect to a railway station, find out his destination, see the train off, and then telephone the police of the town to which he had booked to be on the look-out for him. Apparently it did not occur to the authorities that their quarry might become aware of what was happening and throw off the pursuit by breaking his journey.

On one occasion he was 'seen off' from a naval port, after having taken a ticket for Berlin. But at the first place he alighted, and an hour later was back in the port and free from all surveillance, the local police having satisfied themselves that he was safely on his way to the capital.

At other times he was able to dodge his 'shadow' by expedients so simple that he would have been ashamed to try them on an English village constable, yet they were quite sufficient to baffle the German detectives. His own theory was that German police methods were modelled on the national mentality and temperament, and for that reason, no doubt, were effectual enough when applied to Germans. But the foreigner was a different proposition. He had a disconcerting way of varying his procedure under given conditions, of not acting 'according to plan', and thereby throwing the complicated and elaborate machinery of detection out of gear.

Our informant was convinced that any professional wrong-doer who had served his apprenticeship in England or France might pursue his calling with comparative impunity in Germany until such time as the police had thoroughly familiarised themselves with his methods – and that would be a very long time indeed.

When the German naval authorities joined in the chase for our peripatetic friend they showed no more imagination than the police, and their efforts were equally fruitless. Their tactics were of 'the spider and the fly' order, and they were both surprised and hurt when the fly politely declined to walk into the parlour.

Some two years before the war the agent of whom we are writing received the following letter:

Honoured Sir,

I have heard from a mutual friend that you are interested in the progress and doings of the German fleet. As a retired officer of the navy, I am in a position to give you valuable information, and shall be pleased if you will grant me an interview. I suggest as a rendezvous the ------- Café in the Wilhelmstrasse, where, with a carnation in my buttonhole, I shall be waiting at three p.m. on Thursday.

The signature, it should be added, was illegible.

It is hardly necessary to say that the appointment was not kept, but inquiry soon established the fact that the gentleman with the carnation, so far from being a 'retired officer', was an active captain holding an appointment in the intelligence division of the of the German Admiralty. It was very literally a case of the spider's parlour, for he was waiting in a private room at the café, and in the next apartment were two detectives.

When this ambush failed, a second was set. Another letter came, expressing regret at the agent's non-appearance, pleading for an early meeting, when the writer would be 'happy to disclose information of the most important nature.' To this letter a legible signature was appended, and an address in the suburb of Charlottenburg given. A reply was sent in the following terms:

While thanking you for your kind offer, I would point out that I have no wish to acquire confidential information about the German Navy. This would be equivalent to espionage, which is an offence that exposes one to severe punishment. Such maritime information as I collect is taken from the German press, and is required solely for commercial purposes.

A '*Dienstmann*', or street porter, was despatched with this note to the address given. On arriving at the house he was immediately arrested, taken to the nearest police station, and kept there for several hours, until his captors had satisfied themselves that he knew nothing of the person from whom he had received the note. Incredible as it may sound, three further invitations to meet people who were anxious to disclose information about the German Navy were received by our informant.

Another time his landlady was bullied by the police into making a daily report on her tenant's movements, but the honest woman soon proved unequal to the task, and told him all about it. Twice in his absence were his apartments ransacked for incriminating material that did not exist, and on each occasion the search, though conducted with great secrecy, was made so clumsily that he immediately saw what had occurred.

More to be feared than the German police were would-be coadjutors whose zeal outran their discretion. Our friend was not infrequently approached by British officers, military as a rule, who were spending their leave in Germany and were anxious to do a little independent intelligence work. They were not acting under instructions, but before leaving London they had visited ID headquarters, and had been told where they could find this particular agent.

He, however, by no means relished the role of guide, philosopher, and friend thus thrust upon him. His visitors were almost always very young, very indiscreet, and blissfully ignorant of the elementary rules governing intelligence operations. They were, in fact, a constant source of embarrassment and even danger. Either they would sit in cafés or other public resorts and babble cheerfully of what they intended to do at Kiel or Wilhelmshaven, or – what was still worse – they would move about like stage conspirators, converse in whispers, with furtive glances over the shoulder, pass little notes written in what they fondly believed to be indecipherable code – one habitually used the Greek alphabet! – and generally comport themselves in a manner calculated to arouse the instant suspicion of the most purblind policeman.

'The dear boys made my life a burden,' said our informant:

To this day my hair stands on end when I think of some of their antics. In a weak moment I let one of them accompany me on a visit to Kiel. I went there only to make a few general observations, for when serious work was in hand I preferred to be on my own. But after the first day or two my bright young companion got bored, and went off by himself. He returned to the hotel in the evening, full of excitement and very pleased with himself.

He had spent the day prowling about Gaarden, on the other side of the harbour, where the Krupp-Germania works and the imperial dockyard were situated. He actually presented himself at the main gate of the yard, where a small crowd of visitors were waiting for admission; but learning from the casual remark of a bystander that identity papers had to be shown, he wisely decided to withdraw, and did so rather hurriedly. In a café near by he met two German bluejackets, entered into conversation with them, and found that one of them could speak English. After treating them to several beers, and learning that they belonged to a destroyer undergoing repair in the dockyard, he was invited to visit the boat next day, one of the men promising to meet him at the yard gate at 10 a.m. to escort him inside. My innocent young friend had promptly accepted, and was fully determined to go.

I explained to him, however, that he would be walking straight into an obvious trap. The two sailors knew him to be English – he had, indeed, told them as much – and they must have known also that casual foreigners were never allowed to visit any German naval establishment. To me it was perfectly clear that the men would report the matter to their superiors; that one of them, acting on instructions, would be waiting at the dockyard entrance at the appointed time, and that as soon as my friend passed the turnstile he would be arrested on a charge of espionage.

But I had the utmost difficulty in convincing him of all this, and finally had to threaten to send a strongly worded protest about his indiscreet conduct to the War Office. Most fortunately he had not given his Kiel address to the bluejackets. Even so, I judged it advisable to remove both him and myself from the neighbourhood without delay, and we left Kiel on the next train, thus almost certainly avoiding one of those 'incidents' that the German authorities knew how to exploit so well. Admiral von Tirpitz is credited with the remark that every English 'spy' captured was worth a cruiser to him – meaning that the Reichstag was always more willing to vote money for new ships just after a case of alleged espionage.

A few months after this incident another British Army officer came to me with an introduction. He was a captain in the Royal Garrison Artillery, and was spending a fortnight's leave in Germany. Sitting in the lounge of the Hotel Bristol in Berlin, he outlined his plans to me. He had in his pocket a map showing the defences of Kiel harbour, namely, the batteries at Friedrichsort, Möltenort, and Laboe, with the supposed number and calibre of the guns marked thereon. His intention was to visit these forts in person and check the information on the map.

Quite apart from the extremely hazardous nature of the enterprise – which to my knowledge was, in fact, impossible – I saw at once that he was entirely the wrong sort of man to undertake work of this kind. He was garrulous, excitable, and temperamentally *indiscreet. Often I had to check him when he was beginning to discuss matters that ought not to have been mentioned except behind locked doors.*

He rather resented my attitude, and this made him obstinate when I tried to persuade him to abandon his hare-brained scheme. I pointed out that while his safety was purely his own concern, his inevitable capture – if he persisted in trying to visit the Kiel forts – would not only embarrass the British government, but would also put fresh difficulties in the way of our regular intelligence men, who were already finding the German authorities far more vigilant as a result of these frequent, if always futile, attempts by amateurs to do the work of professional secret service agents.

But all my arguments fell on deaf ears. My companion had made up his mind to go to Kiel, and to Kiel he was going on the morrow. In these circumstances I not only refused to have anything to do with the business, but mentally resolved to put a spoke in his wheel, for the sake of all concerned, his own included.

An hour later a lengthy telegram was despatched, by indirect route, to a certain address in London. The following morning my visitor had a wire, cancelling his leave and directing him to rejoin his regiment forthwith. He was naturally much puzzled and rather angry, but had no suspicion of my connection with the affair. I saw him off by the Hook of Holland express. To this day – assuming him to have survived the war – he is doubtless ignorant of the fact that my cipher telegram to London in all probability saved him from a long term of captivity within the depressing walls of Glatz or Wesel.

After these experiences, which were but two among many of a similar kind, I made strong representations at headquarters as to the imprudence of giving even the mildest official encouragement to amateurs, and, above all, of putting them into touch with me. My own position in Germany was quite precarious enough, and I simply could not afford to incur any risk additional to that which my own work entailed. This protest must have been effectual, for I was not troubled again by indiscreet visitors.

This particular agent had the distinction of becoming an object of special interest to no less a personage than Baron von Kühlmann, the German Chargé d'Affaires in London during the last two years before the war. Acting, no doubt, on instructions from Berlin, the Baron made extensive inquiries in certain circles where he hoped to find people who were personally acquainted with the agent, and who might be persuaded to disclose his whereabouts. These inquiries, however, were conducted with so little finesse that they led to nothing.

One illuminating example of Herr von Kühlmann's diplomatic methods may be cited. He made the acquaintance of a well-known London journalist, invited him to dinner, and there introduced him to two German naval officers, who were visiting England.

'These friends of mine,' he told his guest, 'are very anxious to meet "X" (mentioning the British agent's name), who is believed to be living somewhere in Germany. He seems to be a most interesting person. Do you happen to know where he is to be found?'

This naive gambit immediately put the guest on his guard, and he was careful to give no information whatever. In view of Herr von Kühlmann's reputation for diplomatic astuteness, this incident is worth putting on record.

In pre-war days the German press frequently made more or less overt attacks on members of the British diplomatic corps in central Europe, hinting at illicit activities on their part in the domain of naval and military intelligence work. We have the best authority for declaring these charges to have been utterly baseless. Not only was the conduct of our naval and military attachés at all times scrupulously correct, but for reasons of policy they did not always take advantage of the official facilities for obtaining information that were open to them. They neither met nor corresponded with any intelligence agent, nor did they aid or abet such agents in any way whatsoever.

It would be interesting to know whether all the members of the German diplomatic suite in London during the last pre-war years had an equally impeccable record. There is, at least, strong evidence that not all of them were active in promoting good feeling between the two countries and allaying mutual suspicion. In his well-known book, *The Two White Nations*, Commander Georg von Hase records a conversation he had at Kiel, in July 1914, with the German naval attaché in London, Commander Erich von Müller. This gentleman took Commander von Hase aside, and said to him:

> *Be on your guard against the English: England is ready to fight. We are all on the brink of war. The sole object of this naval visit (of the British Second Battle Squadron) is to spy out the land. They want to get a clear picture of our fleet's readiness for war. Above all, tell them nothing about our submarines.*

Commander von Hase adds that, while this view coincided entirely with his own, he was nevertheless 'astonished to hear it expressed so bluntly'.

It is an interesting fact, not previously divulged, that both

France and Russia maintained a number of naval intelligence agents in Germany. The Russians were the more numerous, and they are understood to have collected a good deal of useful information. There is more than hearsay evidence that several employees of the imperial dockyard at Danzig were Russian agents. If this be true, it would explain the copious and generally accurate data on German submarines that the Russian naval staff possessed on the outbreak of war, for up to that time Danzig was the principal centre for U-boat construction.

Russian agents are also known to have supplied minute details of the German coastal defences in the Baltic, particularly those that guarded the approaches to Königsberg and Danzig. Had the Tsarist fleet been stronger and better led, it might have made good use of this intelligence. But where the Russians really shone was at counter-espionage, some of their achievements in this sphere being noted in another chapter.

As an Irishman might say, the best Russian agents were Poles. Our own intelligence men in Germany sometimes employed Polish helpers, and, as a rule, found them useful and trustworthy. The work attracted them, less on account of the material rewards it brought than of the opportunity it gave them of doing an injury to the power that they regarded as the hereditary oppressor of their distressful country. German-born Poles were invariably the most bitter against their Prussian masters.

Photography, it need hardly be said, plays an important part in intelligence work. The camera often detects details that have escaped the keenest eye and, for this reason, our agents in Germany did their utmost to secure photographs of every new ship at the earliest possible moment. Sometimes as many as a dozen views were obtained, all taken from different angles. One of our agents succeeded in getting snapshots of the battlecruiser *Derff-linger* as she lay on the building slip, and these revealed certain features of her underbody that had hitherto been unsuspected.

It is safe to say that we had detailed photographs of every German warship afloat in August 1914, the pictures being filed at ID headquarters in chronological sequence, so that the changes in rig and general appearances, due to dockyard refit, could be noted at a glance. In this way the admiralty draughtsmen were able to prepare meticulously accurate silhouettes of every German fighting craft, thereby facilitating their identification if met with at sea.

Not long before the war a solitary German ship, the *Blücher,* was fitted with a tripod foremast of British pattern. Within a week after emerging from dockyard with her new mast she had been photographed, and the existing silhouette of the ship corrected accordingly.

Incidentally this mast was responsible for the death of many German sailors in the Dogger Bank action, for when the *Blücher* was sinking she was mistaken by a Zeppelin for a British ship, and bombs were dropped. This attack compelled our destroyers engaged in rescue work to draw off, with the result that hundreds of Germans in the water had to be left to their fate.

Those who have been associated with intelligence work are the first to appreciate the profound psychology of Poe's 'Purloined Letter'. Alike in concealment and detection, the simpler the methods employed, the greater the probability of success. Elsewhere we have paid a tribute to the effectiveness of the censorship that Germany imposed on naval news as a retort to Lord Fisher's 'hush' policy. But while it is true that this censorship kept us in the dark for several years, the elaborate secrecy in which the Germans sought to cloak every naval development, important and otherwise, often had an effect the reverse of what was intended.

Time after time our intelligence agents were put on the track of some highly important event by the ostentatious measures taken to conceal it. Cases in point were the *Blücher-Elsass* gunnery experiment, and the building of the first German 15-inch gun. We got wind of the latter even before it had been tested on the Krupp proving grounds at Meppen, simply because of the almost theatrical precautions with which it was surrounded.

Precisely the same thing happened in connection with the engines for *U-19*, the first submarine to be fitted with Diesel machinery. Their construction at the Krupp-Germania works in Kiel would have remained unknown but for the fact that the particular shop where they were being assembled was barricaded off from the others and plastered with notices threatening trespassers with dire penalties. Inevitably, therefore, it was soon spread about the whole works that something of a highly secret nature was in progress, and as the firm employed 6,000 hands, the news quickly circulated throughout Kiel. Being thus provided with a definite clue, one of our secret service men followed it up, and eventually obtained full details of the new engine.

In February 1912 the Kaiser's speech at the opening of the Reichstag clearly foreshadowed new legislation for increasing the navy. It was very important for this country to learn what was impending, for at that date British naval policy was necessarily governed to a great extent by developments across the North Sea. Although the new bill was not presented to the Reichstag until 14 June, its substance was communicated to British ID headquarters early in May. This was the work of an enterprising agent who secured, by very simple means, a set of proofs from the establishment where copies of the bill were being printed for distribution to the Reichstag deputies.

It is not surprising that the disclosure caused a sensation in London, for the new legislative measure was designed to raise the German fleet to a level of strength far above anything previously anticipated. Provision was made for an eventual establishment of forty-one battleships, twenty battlecruisers, forty light cruisers, 144 destroyers, and seventy-two submarines, or more than twice as many modern fighting ships – barring destroyers – as Germany possessed in 1914. These figures, we may observe in parentheses, should leave no doubt as to the reality or the gravity of the German naval menace in the days of which we are writing. Looking back at that period, it is amazing that so many people in England, including some of our most intelligent public men, should have remained blind to the numerous and unmistakable portents of war that were crowding on the horizon. If Armageddon caught us partly unprepared it was not for lack of warning.

CHAPTER 7

WHY JUTLAND WAS INDECISIVE

IT IS USELESS to pretend that the British nation was wholly satisfied with the naval operations of the Great War. There still exists a widespread belief that the incomparable resources we possessed, both personal and material, for the conduct of sea warfare were neither sufficiently exploited nor always employed to the best advantage.

No doubt the great mass of the British public failed to appreciate the peculiar and, indeed, unique conditions that governed the naval campaign. Having unbounded confidence in the navy – a confidence that never stood higher than in August 1914, despite the 'panics' and the professional controversies within the service itself, which were so marked a feature of the decade preceding the war – it looked for a succession of brilliant victories at sea, worthy to rank with the most glorious achievements of the Nelsonic era.

Instead, there came reports of indecisive actions, and, more than once, of actual defeats at the hands of an enemy who was known to be greatly inferior in strength. Almost the only major events of the war at sea that roused the nation to enthusiasm were the spirited raid on the Bight of Heligoland on 28 August 1914, the annihilation of Von Spee's squadron off the Falklands a few months later, and the heroic attack on Zeebrugge on St George's Day, 1918.

True, the Dogger Bank action in January 1915 was a victory so far as it went, but subsequent information left no doubt that a great opportunity had been missed.

Jutland was for the British public the crowning disappointment. Here, for the first time, the Grand Fleet and the High Seas Fleet came into contact and fought a pitched battle. Strategically it was indecisive, except in so far as it confirmed the command of the sea surface that Great Britain had exercised from the beginning of the war. A whole library has been written about this engagement. Scores of German authors have attempted to prove that Jutland was a signal triumph for their fleet. On the British side there has been endless controversy, some writers maintaining that we scored a victory more or less decisive, others that it was a drawn battle with honours evenly divided, and a few who refer to it as a 'disaster'.

These contradictory opinions do not appear to have had much effect on the average citizen. Unversed in the niceties of strategy and tactics, he has weighed the visible results and found them less than he expected. On the plain evidence before him he sees no grounds for claiming a victory. The Grand Fleet went into action with a margin of superiority in tonnage and gun power that could fairly be described as overwhelming. In the opening phase six British battlecruisers fought five German ships of similar type, the former having a decided preponder-ance in weight of gunfire. Yet within an hour two of our ships were destroyed and at least one other was severely damaged, while the German squadron remained intact, with all its ships still in fighting trim.

In the second phase, the German battle fleet was engaged two hours with our main fleet under circumstances distinctly unfavourable to the enemy. Caught in what was, by all the rules of the game, a hopeless trap, and exposed to a concentrated fire of hundreds of the heaviest guns mounted afloat, Admiral Scheer contrived to extricate himself with comparatively trivial losses, and, eventually, to regain his base without being brought to action a second time. Such, baldly stated, were the results of the battle as the man in the street sees them. Whatever the conclusions to be drawn, the facts themselves are incontestable.

It is not proposed to deal here with questions of leadership or strategy. We shall confine ourselves to an examination of cer-tain material factors that played an extremely important part at Jutland and in other actions of the war, and that, we believe, will shed new light on many incidents that have long mystified the public.

Save for certain characteristics in profile and rig, there was little outward difference between British and German capital ships before the war. But appearances were in this case deceptive.

When Germany, following the example set by Great Brit-ain, began to build dreadnoughts, she designed them chiefly for the purpose of operating at a relatively short distance from their home bases. They were, therefore, ships with a limited radius of action, not only with regard to fuel supply, but also in respect of accommodation for the personnel. Habitability was quite a minor consideration, for the ships were not intended to remain at sea for lengthy periods or to undertake long voyages. The crews, in fact, were meant to live ashore except when the fleet was exercising, and to this end enormous barracks were erected at Kiel and Wilhelmshaven.

To put the matter in an expressive though exaggerated form, German battleships were floating batteries with emergency accommodation for the crew. British battleships, on the other hand, were built to sail and fight in any part of the globe where their presence might be required, and it was therefore essential to provide generous living quarters for the health and reasonable comfort of the personnel.

This fundamental difference between German and British principles of construction goes far towards explaining the remarkable powers of enduring punishment, which German ships exhibited in action. Being free to dispense with the large berthing spaces, which were so necessary a feature of British ships, the German constructor was able to sub-divide his hull into numerous, small, watertight compartments that localised damage sustained below the waterline by shell fire, torpedo or gun.

The value of this method of protection was demonstrated by the number of German capital ships that remained afloat, and in many cases still capable of fighting, after they had received underwater injuries. Particulars are as follows:

Westfalen, 1 torpedo;
Ostfriesland, 1 mine;
Grosser Kurfürst, 1 mine;
Markgraf, 2 mines;

Kronprinz, 1 torpedo;

Bayern, 1 mine;

Moltke, 2 torpedoes;

Goeben, 5 mines;

Seydlitz, 1 mine and 1 torpedo.

As we have stated elsewhere, the robust protection of the German ships was no secret to the British Admiralty. It was the theme of many secret service reports, often accompanied by drawings that showed the entire system of watertight compartments.

The armour plating of these ships was also very extensive and massive. Every tonne saved by the mounting of relatively light-weight guns and by other economies of weight in construction and equipment was put into armour defence.

As the ships spent little time at sea, the ventilation question was not of prime importance, and it was thus possible to plate up the sides of the hull where, in British vessels, lines of portholes (scuttles) were an absolute necessity. Germany, there-fore, had a fleet of dreadnoughts, which were as unsinkable as human ingenuity could make them. That they were cramped, ill-ventilated, and uncomfortable mattered little in view of their clearly defined purpose, which was to fight in the North Sea, the Baltic, and perhaps in the Channel, but at no greater dis-tance from the Heligoland Bight. Regarded purely as combative units, irrespective of radius and strategical mobility, they were undoubtedly superior to their British contemporaries.

Now, although it would have been bad policy on our part to have built our dreadnoughts as 'floating batteries' on the German principle, having regard to our world-wide strategical commit-ments, it nevertheless lay within our power to counter by other means the tactical advantage that the Germans derived from the superior defensive properties of their ships.

When, indeed, the two fleets were compared on paper, it looked as though we had taken the needful steps in that direction, for our ships carried much heavier guns. Against the German 11-inch and 12-inch, we matched 13.5-inch and 15-inch weapons. In theory, the latter were powerful enough to crush the German ships in spite of their thick armour, and in practice they would certainly have done so had we used the right kind of shell.

Unfortunately, while we built great guns and neglected to provide them with efficient projectiles, Germany built smaller guns, but supplied them with shells of superlative quality.

The consequence was that in actual destructive power the German medium-calibre weapons were equal, if not superior, to our heavier ordnance, and so, on balance, the German ships enjoyed a net advantage by virtue of their stronger protection.

We know from the statements of von Tirpitz and other German authorities that they made a careful study of the protective features of British ships, and then designed their own guns and projectiles with a special view to attacking these prospective targets in the most effective manner. The principles that actuated the respective naval ordnance policies of Britain and Germany are much too technical to be examined in detail, but they may be briefly indicated in terms that need not affright the non-professional reader.

Both powers had made an exhaustive study of the gunnery data provided by the Russo-Japanese War of 1904–5, but the inferences they drew were by no means parallel.

In the opinion of British experts, the annihilation of the Russian fleet at Tsushima was due to the high-explosive shell used by the Japanese heavy guns. These projectiles had thin walls, an abnormally large bursting charge, and extremely sensitive fuses. Very few of them penetrated the armour of the Russian ships. The majority detonated against the sides, decks, and superstructure.

A vivid picture of the havoc they wrought is given by Capt. Vladimir Semenoff in his narrative of the battle, together with some notes on the subject of projectiles, which are very pertinent to our present theme:

> It seemed as if these (the Japanese projectiles) were mines, not shells, which were striking the ship's side and falling on the deck. They burst as soon as they touched anything – the moment they encountered the least impediment in their flight.
>
> Handrails, funnel guys, topping lifts of the boats' derricks, were quite sufficient to cause a thoroughly efficient burst. The steel plates and superstructure on the upper deck were torn to pieces ... Iron ladders were crumpled up into rings, and guns were literally hurled from their mountings. Such havoc would never be caused by the simple impact of a shell, still less by that of its splinters. It could only be caused by the force of the explosion.

In a footnote he adds:

> For a great many years in naval gunnery two distinct ideas have prevailed: one is to inflict on the enemy, although not necessarily much (in quantity), severe and heavy damage – i.e. to stop movement, to penetrate under the waterline, to get a burst in the hull below the waterline, briefly, to put the ship at once out of action; the other is to pour upon him the greatest volume of fire in the shortest

time, though it be above water and the actual damage caused by each individual shot be immaterial, in the hope of paralysing the ship, trusting that if this were done it would not be difficult to destroy her completely – that she would, in fact, sink by herself.

With modern guns, in order to secure the first of the above ideas, solid armour-penetrating projectiles must be employed – i.e. thick-coated shells (whose internal capacity and bursting charge are consequently diminished), and percussion fuses with retarded action, bursting the shell inside the target. To secure the second idea, shells need only be sufficiently solid to ensure their not bursting at the moment of being fired. The thickness of their walls may be reduced to the minimum, and their internal capacity and bursting charge increased to the utmost limits. The percussion fuses should be sensitive enough to detonate at the slightest touch.

The first of the above views prevails chiefly in France, the second in England. In the late war we (Russia) held the first, and the Japanese the second.

There is scarcely any room for doubt that Lord Fisher had what he conceived to be the true moral of Tsushima in mind when he initiated the dreadnought policy. He visualised a battleship with multiple big guns pouring a stream of highly explosive shells, with instant-impact fuses, into the target, blowing away all the unarmoured parts, and reducing it to a mere hulk without necessarily penetrating the belt armour. Such of the crew as escaped death or wounds would be demoralised by this hurricane of flame and splintered steel, and although the ship might still float, she would no longer exist as a fighting organism.

Nor was this policy modified when we increased the calibre of our guns from 12-inch to 13.5-inch, and then to 15-inch. It is true that a certain proportion of the shells were armour-piercing ones, but reliance was placed chiefly on the high-explosive type that the Japanese had used with such terrible effect at Tsushima.

Our policy would have been sound enough had the German battleships of 1914 resembled in construction and armour defence the ill-starred Russian vessels of 1905; but, in fact, they were built on entirely different lines.

Unlike the Russian pre-dreadnoughts, with their thin belt of armour and vast area of thinly or non-protected sides, the German dreadnoughts were 'stiff' with armour on the waterline and well above it, the side plating being conjoined with thick steel decks and armoured bulkheads, running fore and aft and athwart ships. Every gun position, every control station, every place in the ship where a hit might cause serious injury, was sheathed in armour, against which shells might burst harmlessly as long as they did not penetrate.

Clearly, therefore, the type of projectile that had turned the scale at Tsushima was quite unsuitable for attacking such ships as these. Possessing, as we did, almost complete details of the protection of every German dreadnought, it is difficult to understand why we failed to develop a thoroughly efficient armour-piercing shell – one, that is, that would perforate thick armour and burst inside with devastating violence.

The qualities demanded of such a projectile are lucidly set forth in a later passage, descriptive of the shells that the Germans fired at Jutland.

Here it may be asserted on the best authority that our leading armament firms were prepared, long before the war, to turn out armour-piercing shells that were fully equal to the German type. They were not invited to do so, and the result was that much of the work of our Grand Fleet gunners at Jutland was rendered abortive by the indifferent penetrative and explosive properties of the shells they had to use. Many of the 15-inch projectiles fired at the German ships were actually filled with ordinary gunpowder, which gave a comparatively feeble detonation. Had they been charged with lyddite, or, better still, with TNT, every hit we made would have been twice as destructive. In view of the number of hits scored during the battle by our heaviest guns, it may be confidently affirmed that only the inferior quality of our shells saved the German fleet from partial destruction.

To attempt to fix the responsibility for this grave defect in our naval material would be futile. How easily it might have been remedied is made clear by Lord Jellicoe, who has related in his book on the Grand Fleet how, soon after Jutland, a committee was appointed to investigate the shell question. Owing to the recommendations of this committee, a new and thoroughly efficient type of armour-piercing projectile was developed, which would penetrate thick armour even when striking it at an oblique angle, pass through intact, and, thanks to a reliable delay-action fuse, detonate inside with most destructive results.

The failure to provide such a shell before the war was probably due to want of practical experience of heavy gunfire against targets representing well-armoured ships. This could only be gained by experiments such as the Germans conducted. They spent large sums in building targets that reproduced sections of the armoured hull of a modern battleship, and attacked them at sea with various types of projectiles, fired under the most realistic conditions possible. By this method they secured data that enabled them to produce a shell that could be relied upon to function with maximum efficiency. There was no reason why we should not have carried out similar experiments. That we did not do so is a serious reflection on the pre-war Boards of Admiralty. This neglect almost certainly cost us a decisive victory at Jutland, and on other occasions largely neutralised our advantage in heavy artillery.

The North Sea skirmish of 17 November 1917 furnished a glaring example. In a running fight with enemy light cruisers HMS *Repulse* scored a raking hit on the *Königsberg*. A 15-inch shell, weighing 1,920 lb, passed through the bases of all three funnels and burst in one of the forward coal bunkers. So feeble was the detonation that the shell fell apart in a few large fragments, and caused only local damage that in no wise impaired the efficiency of the ship. Had this projectile been filled with TNT it would probably have blown the bottom out of the *Königsberg*, or at least have disabled her.

Apart from the material evidence furnished by the summary destruction of five large British ships, the efficacy of the German shells is attested by many witnesses. As a rule they passed through strong armour and burst with terrific violence, causing widespread damage and very severe casualties.

By way of contrast we may cite a German witness on the behaviour of the British projectiles. Herr Betzhold, writing in '*Die Technik im Weltkriege*', offers the following comment:

> *The effects of heavy hits on the German ships showed clearly that the British ammunition was inferior. Their projectiles in part did not burst at all, and in part detonated outside the armour; while the German fuse did not produce an explosion until the shell had passed through the armour. The composition and stowage of the*

British powder charges, and their inadequate protection, consti-
tuted an ever-present source of danger to the whole ship. Both in
disposition and thickness the British armour proved unequal to
the attack of the medium-calibre German guns; on the other hand,
the strength and quality of the German armour were such as to
defeat attack by the heaviest British calibres. The 15-inch shell was
unable to penetrate our thirteen and three quarter-inch armour
even at ranges from 6 to 9.25 miles.

Herr Betzhold's claim as to the superiority of the German armour was not borne out by experiments made after the war. Plates taken from the surrendered battleship *Baden* were found, when subjected to tests, to be definitely inferior in resisting power to British armour of the same thickness; but these tests, it is to be assumed, were made with the post-Jutland type of British armour-piercing projectiles.

Since the war full details have been released of the German type of shell used at Jutland. As the agency directly responsi-ble for the sinking of our three battlecruisers – *Queen Mary, Indefatigable, Invincible* – not to mention the destruction of three armoured cruisers and the heavy damage inflicted on other vessels, this deadly projectile deserves some notice. For the fol-lowing particulars we are indebted to Commander Kinzel, an officer who served before the war in the ordnance department of the German Navy Office.

Long before the war, he states, his department had realised the importance of improving armour-piercing projectiles, and had devoted endless thought and experiment to the subject. In collaboration with the Krupp firm, the work had gone on for many years, regardless of difficulties and disappointments, and was eventually crowned with such success that by the outbreak of war a comparatively perfect AP shell had been evolved.

The body of the shell consisted of Krupp's crucible, nickel-chrome steel, unsurpassed in toughness and hardness. The shell tapered at the nose to a long and fine point, which would have broken off when impacting on armour but for the protection afforded by the cap, made of softer material.

The discovery of the most favourable form and the most suitable material for this cap was only made after numerous experiments that cost a great deal of money. At the base of the shell an opening was provided for the introduction of the bursting-charge, the weight of which was about 3 per cent of that of the entire projectile. To obtain the maximum effect from the burst it was necessary to employ a highly explosive aromatic composition; but since substances of this nature were liable to detonate immediately upon impact against armour, there arose for solution the difficult problem of so 'phlegmatising' the charge that it could be brought safely through the thickest armour, though without in any way impairing the violence of its disruption.

'The severity of this problem,' writes Commander Kinzel,

May be adjudged by the fact that at the date of the Jutland action the British had not succeeded in solving it. In spite of prolonged experiments, they had been compelled to load their armour-piercing shell almost exclusively with black powder, which, although less sensitive, was far less efficient than the high-explosive compounds.'

The fuse has been aptly described as the 'soul' of the shell. To design a delay-action fuse that will function perfectly in an AP projectile is in itself a most difficult problem. It must occupy the minimum of weight and space. The minute elements of which it is composed must be proof against the sudden shock of discharge, for the premature detonation of a shell within the bore would wreck the gun, kill the turret crew, and, by probably igniting the ready cartridges inside the turret, gravely imperil the ship.

It is further essential that those elements should withstand the tremendous concussion that results when the shell impinges on the armoured target. This is the instant at which the fuse becomes active and, in due course, causes the charge to explode.

> *Thanks to an unwearying devotion to duty [adds our informant] which rose superior to the innumerable disappointments that were met with, we succeeded at length in devising a delay-action fuse that was unaffected by any shock, allowed the intact projectile to penetrate well into the vitals of a hostile ship and then caused it to detonate. In this way, therefore, was put into the hands of the German Navy an armour-piercing shell as perfect as human skill could make it – a weapon superior to anything that our opponents possessed.*

After due allowance has been made for the patriotic exuberance of Commander Kinzel, it must be acknowledged that the German projectiles were more effective than our own. But as soon as one begins to inquire into the cause of this deficiency on our part, many contradictory statements are encountered.

It is asserted, for example, that the admiralty insisted on using, or trying to use, lyddite as a filling for armour-piercing shells, and that, as this compound was found to be too sensitive for the purpose, black powder had to be substituted. Other, and more technical reasons, have been advanced to account for the comparative failure of our projectiles against German armour.

From naval officers, however, a simpler explanation has been forthcoming, which tends to confirm the observations already made as to the principles that governed the admiralty's ordnance policy down to the date of Jutland. One of these officers has been quoted as saying:

> *We knew long before Jutland that our AP shell was bad. Efforts were made to improve it, but the answer always came that high-explosives were 'the stuff to give them'; that the smashing, racking, and wrenching effects of high-explosive shell would tear the strongest-armoured ship to pieces before she had a single clean perforation of her belt. This, I believe, was the substance of reports from our people in Japan during the war with Russia, and we assumed that the German dreadnoughts would prove no less vulnerable to high-explosive attack then Rojestvensky's ships had done. As a result, the powers that be did not persevere with the attempt to produce a thoroughly effective armour-piercing shell. That we could have done so had we persisted is evident from the fact that an almost perfect projectile was being produced not many months after Jutland.*

Apart from the ammunition question, the test of war revealed further shortcomings in British naval equipment. Our range-finders and other optical instruments necessary for fire-control purposes were inferior to those used in the German fleet, as has been officially admitted. Why they were inferior has still to be explained. In the early part of the Jutland action, at any rate, the German fire was more accurate than our own. The rapidity with which the enemy's ships found the range and began hitting was a painful surprise to Admiral Jellicoe himself. It was the more astonishing because, at the date of Jutland, the Germans had not installed a director-control system, such as most of our capital ships already possessed, that was supposed to increase very considerably the accuracy of gunfire.

The effects of the German shooting were enhanced by their method of 'bunching' salvoes. Their guns were so calibrated that all the shots from a broadside pitched in a very small area. If, therefore, the aim were accurate, the target was liable to be struck by several shells at once. This happened to the *Queen Mary* and other ships we lost, and serves to explain the appalling suddenness with which they were obliterated.

On the other hand, unless the aim were absolutely correct, 'bunched' salvoes missed the target clean.

British guns were not so closely calibrated, and by comparison with the German broadsides ours appeared to be 'ragged', some shots pitching short of, and others over, the target. This method of firing was deliberate, the idea being to increase the chances of hitting by giving each salvo a fairly wide spread, a single hit being rightly adjudged better than none at all.

Each system had its merits and disadvantages so well balanced that there was little to choose between the two methods. The Germans, however, might well claim to have profited by Lord Fisher's metaphor: if you are insulted at the dinner-table, don't throw the decanter stopper at the offender: throw the decanter. They certainly threw with deadly effect in the battlecruiser action at Jutland.

Irrespective of calibre, there were notable differences between the British and German big guns. The former, built on the wire-wound system, were exceedingly heavy for their bore, our 15-inch weighing nearly 100 tonnes unmounted. The German guns were of the all-steel pattern, and very much lighter, their

15-inch weighing little more than 70 tonnes; yet in accuracy they were by no means inferior to our weapons, and were much longer lived.

On the outbreak of war the ships of both navies had inadequate protection against the risk of shell-flash reaching the magazines. Luckily for the Germans, they discovered this grave danger sixteen months before Jutland, and were able to take the necessary precautions in time. In the Dogger Bank action of January 1915, the two after-turrets of the battlecruiser *Seydlitz* were converted into raging furnaces by a single British shell that fractured the base of the aftermost turret and sent white-hot splinters into the ammunition hoist, igniting several cartridges.

Nitro-cellulose powder burns with intense fury. The flames shot up and down the hoist, found their way through a communicating trap to the second turret, and started a similar blaze there. One hundred and sixty men perished in this holocaust, and only the heroic action of a petty officer, who closed a hatch in the nick of time, prevented the fire from reaching the magazines. Following this experience, anti-flash doors were fitted to all important ships, and other measures taken went far towards eliminating the danger.

Another safety factor on the German side was represented by the brass cartridge cases in which the main powder charges for the big guns were contained, only the secondary charges being packed in silk bags. Thus, when shell flashes entered a turret or an ammunition hoist, the main charges, being sheathed in brass, rarely caught fire. In the British Navy, all powder charges were enclosed in silk, and were therefore much more liable to be touched off by a flash.

The poor quality of our pre-war mines has been mentioned in

a previous chapter. Although the characteristics of the German mine were well known to the admiralty, no attempt was made to produce an equally efficient weapon, and so, for the first half of the war, our elaborate minelaying operations were to a great extent wasted energy.

The point we wish to drive home is this: it was not for want of advance information as to the details of German naval equipment that we neglected to provide ourselves with material equally good. The secret service agent's job was done when he had gathered this information and, after verifying it as far as possible, forwarded it to the proper quarter. If it were not made use of, the blame did not rest with him.

Whatever the explanation may be – absence of a proper naval staff or excessive conservatism in high administrative circles – there remains the inexorable fact that our pre-war Navy, despite its splendid ships and incomparable personnel, was lacking in certain material elements that were absolutely vital to complete fighting efficiency. The absence of these was responsible for more than one tragedy of lost endeavour.

CHAPTER 8

SOME NOTABLE 'SCOOPS'

MODERN NAVAL WARFARE is so complicated a business that it can be waged only by specialists. That, of course, is a truism, but we are writing here with reference to the actual weapons employed, not to strategy or leadership. Each weapon has its ardent devotees. The torpedo specialist likes to think of his beloved 'tin fish' as the most potent engines of destruction afloat, and, incidentally, his conviction – or obsession – on this point is largely responsible for the extreme complexity of the modern large warship. There are even naval officers, mainly of junior rank, who think that aircraft will eventually dominate the surface of the sea.

But the navy as a whole prefers the gun to all other weapons, and with reason. It was the arm that decided every important action of the Great War – Heligoland Bight, Dogger Bank, Coronel, the Falklands, and Jutland.

The battleship is essentially a floating platform for big guns, and when we increase her tonnage, her speed, and her armour protection, we do so only in order to enlarge her capacity for carrying big guns, to give the platform greater mobility, and to render it less vulnerable to counter-attack. In a word, the ship exists for the gun, not the gun for the ship.

Hence the supreme importance that is almost universally attached to gunnery.

Some account has been given in the previous chapter of the extraordinary pains that the Germans took to develop an efficient shell for their heavy guns, and of the spectacular results it produced at Jutland. But unless accurately aimed, the best projectile is wasted. We shall now disclose the methods by which the German Navy attained its high standard of gunnery, and how, in due course, these jealously guarded secrets were penetrated by the British secret service.

Long after the high-powered naval breech-loading gun had been introduced, target practice in every navy was still conducted at comparatively short range. Although the gun itself could throw its projectile with accuracy up to a very considerable distance, its powers in this respect were not exploited – for the sufficient reason that no system of controlling fire at long range had been evolved.

But in the nineties of last century certain progressive naval officers in this country and elsewhere began to demonstrate the possibility of long-range gunfire, having first devised, quite independently of one another, the requisite instruments. The four men chiefly responsible for initial progress in this direction were Admiral Sir Percy Scott, Admirals Fiske and Simms in the United States, and Admiral Thomsen in Germany.

In each case the telescopic sight was the prime element in

the new system. Using this in conjunction with the 'dotter', 'deflection teacher', and other devices invented by himself, Scott obtained astonishing results with the guns of successive ships he commanded. He also revived the old method of broadside 'parallel firing', by which the axes of all guns bearing on the broadside are so adjusted as to give the weapons a common point of aim. This was the genesis of salvo firing, as distinct from independent shooting.

Finally he invented the director system that bears his name. This enables one man to aim and fire all the guns in the ship. If his aim be accurate – and it depends not merely on his own skill, but on that of the colleague who is 'spotting' the fall of shot from a masthead position, and also on abstruse mathematical calculations that are being made in the 'transmitting station' deep in the bowels of the ship – the target may be hit by a full broadside, just as the smallest miscalculation or error of judgement will cause all the shots to miss the mark.

Under the inspiration of Admiral Thomsen, the German Navy began experimental practice at long ranges in 1895. In the following year a concentration shoot by battle squadrons was carried out near Swinemünde, in the presence of the Kaiser, who was so impressed by the results that he exerted his personal influence to secure the steady development of long-distance gunnery in the fleet.

A new navy is apt to be less conservative than one of older standing, and thus it was that, in Germany, every innovation that promised to increase the fighting efficiency of the fleet was assured beforehand of official encouragement. In England, unfortunately, it was too often the other way about, inventors and would-be reformers having an uphill fight to gain official recognition.

The Germans, having proved long-range firing to be practicable, at once proceeded to give their naval guns an extremely high angle of elevation. The importance of this needs a word of explanation. Within certain limits, the higher the angle at which a gun is fired, the further the shot will travel. A 12-inch gun firing at 15 degrees will throw its shot 16,000 yards, but if the muzzle is raised to 30 degrees the extreme range will be increased to 24,000 yards.

As the Germans, as far back as 1900, were giving their turret guns an elevation of 30 degrees, while the guns of contemporary British ships were limited to 13 and a half, it follows that the German vessels outranged ours by a very substantial margin. Had war broken out at that period, the German fleet would have enjoyed an immense, perhaps a decisive, advantage by its two-fold superiority in range and accuracy of fire.

Although we soon got wind of the German high-angle mountings, their significance appears to have been minimised, probably because we knew little or nothing about the quality of the German fleet's gunnery. Our ignorance on this subject persisted until a very few years before the outbreak of war, but from time to time scraps of information percolated through which, when pieced together, made it clear that our prospective enemies were leaving nothing undone to improve their naval marksmanship. An intelligence agent in 1909 drew attention to the high rate of fire of which the German guns seemed to be capable, the 11-inch discharging three, and the 9.4-inch four, rounds a minute. This rapidity could not be equalled by the main armament of British battleships.

When Germany designed her first dreadnoughts she took occasion to overhaul her gunnery system. Numerous and costly experiments were made with new methods of fire control, the best elements of each being subsequently incorporated in a standard system with which all the newer ships were equipped. This, the 'Richtungsweiser', or direction pointer, had certain features in common with those of the Scott director, though in other respects the rival systems were dissimilar.

Of director control, as understood in the British Navy, the German fleet had none *until a year after the Battle of Jutland*, yet the brilliance of its gunnery in that action was attested by the results.

They were the natural fruits of twenty years of intensive work, carried on with characteristic German perseverance and thoroughness. For every hundred pounds we spent on gunnery research and experiment during this period, Germany spent a thousand. To give but one example: secret service agents in 1910 disclosed that the ammunition allowance for practice purposes was on a far more generous scale than that of the British fleet, the number of rounds per heavy gun being 80 per cent higher. Practice with 'live' shell against armoured targets was quite a common occurrence, though it was rarely, if ever, indulged in by the British Navy.

These facts are adduced to show that there was nothing miraculous in the accuracy of German naval gunfire. The guns themselves and their projectiles were of first-class quality, it is true, but the almost uniformly high standard of shooting was the perfection that is only born of unremitting practice.

From the secret service point of view, gunnery data were valued more highly than almost any other class of information, and for fairly obvious reasons they were very difficult to obtain. There were several ways of securing details of a new ship, a new gun, or a new torpedo. For example, by accepting certain risks the agent might procure what he wanted by personally visiting a dockyard or an ordnance factory. But while such visits were, in fact, not infrequently made, it was a very different matter to go on board a foreign warship and watch her carry out firing exercises.

Oddly enough, the only secret agent who is supposed to have performed this feat was working on behalf of the United States. According to letters exchanged between two American naval officers – and, apparently with their permission, published in the American press in 1925 – an American contrived to be on board a British battleship when she was engaged in long-range practice, and noted that the anti-torpedo bulges on one side were flooded to give her a list, thus increasing the elevation of her guns. Neither the dale nor any other details of the incident were given, and it is quite possibly apocryphal.

Be that as it may, no British agent in Germany ever claimed to have effected as dramatic a coup. Nevertheless, by employing less direct methods we were able to get more than one glimpse of German naval gunnery, which ought to have left us in no doubt as to its quality.

The introduction of high-angle mountings in the German fleet has already been mentioned. Actual photographs were obtained, depicting pre-dreadnoughts of the *Deutschland* and *Braunschweig* class with their turret guns cocked up at acute angles.

We knew, too, that several of these ships had carried out 'bombardment' shoots at ranges up to 14,000 yards, the targets being stationary and the ranges plotted to advance.

This item of news was valuable as confirmation of the long range of German guns, but it had no other significance, for in those days (1907), and for several years afterwards, the High Seas Fleet never exceeded a range of 10,000 yards when firing at moving targets. In Germany, as in this country, shooting at any greater distance was regarded as a waste of powder and shot.

When the first German dreadnoughts were laid down it was naturally inferred that their guns would have an angle of elevation at least as high as that in the earlier ships. In fact, our original intelligence reports on the *Nassau* and *Helgoland* class credited their big guns with 30 degrees of elevation. The truth was not discovered until the ships had been in commission for some time. It was then found that their mountings permitted an elevation of only 16 degrees.

What had happened was this. The 11-inch and 12-inch guns with which the German dreadnoughts were armed were of exceptionally high velocity. They were designed for flat trajectory fire, and consequently their range, even at a very moderate degree of elevation, was far beyond that at which accurate aiming was considered to be feasible. It was therefore deemed pointless to give them an elevation above 16 degrees – equivalent to about 19,500 yards' range – especially as high-angle mountings were heavier, more complicated, and more expensive than the other type, and also necessitated a larger gun port, this latter tendering the turret more vulnerable to shell splinters.

From 1907 to the end of the Great War Germany built and completed twenty-six dreadnought battleships and battlecruisers, their guns in every case having a maximum elevation of 16 degrees. Within the same period we built and completed nearly forty similar ships, all but ten of which (the 12-inch gun ships) had a maximum gun elevation of 20 degrees. Thus, while Germany was lowering the elevation of her big naval guns, we were raising that of our own weapons, the procedure in each case having been dictated by practical reasons.

In our own case the step up from 15 to 20 degrees was made necessary by the introduction of the 13.5-inch gun. As this piece had a lower muzzle velocity than the 12-inch, it became advisable to give it a higher angle of elevation in order to maintain equality of range. As, during most of this time, target practice in both fleets continued to be carried out at an extreme range of 10,000 yards, the difference in their gun-elevation standards appeared to be a matter of small moment.

To anticipate matters, it may here be remarked that this difference proved to be of great importance. From 1911 onward the development of long-range fire was extraordinarily rapid, and during the war hits were made at distances almost twice as great as the average target-practice range of pre-war days. In many British narratives of the naval campaign emphasis is laid on the supposedly superior range of the German big guns. The late Sir Percy Scott himself fell into this error. The truth is that at Jutland our ships as a whole definitely outranged those of the enemy, and in more than one phase of the action held them under a galling fire to which they could offer no reply, owing to the limited elevation of their guns.

In 1910 some important experiments were carried out in the Baltic with the Direction-Pointer system of fire control, the ships concerned being the *Nassau* and *Westfalen*. It was then demonstrated that a fair percentage of hits could be obtained on moving targets at ranges exceeding 12,000 yards, and after certain improvements had been made in the system further practical tests were arranged. Our intelligence men at that period made frequent references to this pronounced activity in the sphere of fleet gunnery, but of reliable and detailed information there was little or none. All that we knew for certain was that the Germans were doing their utmost to develop long-range shooting; of the actual results we remained in ignorance.

But in March 1911 definite and very illuminating information was obtained.

It described an experimental shoot by a division of German 11-inch gun ships. At ranges averaging 12,500 yards they had scored 8 per cent of hits on a towed target, the sea being rather choppy, and visibility only moderately good.

These results were so far in advance of anything previously recorded that British experts were at first inclined to be sceptical, but corroborative evidence was soon forthcoming. Thereafter our secret service redoubled its efforts to keep in touch with the progress of German gunnery. At some risk, and after the exercise of much ingenuity and endless patience, certain avenues of communication were opened by means of which we hoped to secure the desired intelligence. The precise nature of the means employed cannot be disclosed even now.

In April 1911 one of our agents in Germany got wind of a coming cruise by a 'special service' division, consisting of the battleship *Elsass*, the armoured cruiser *Blücher*, and a light cruiser. Discreet inquiries left no doubt as to the purpose of this undertaking. Even before the ships left Kiel it was known that twenty officers, all of whom were gunnery experts, had been specially detailed to make this cruise, and that with them was the deputy chief of the *Waffen-Abteilung* (ordnance department) of the German Admiralty and two high officials from the firm of Krupp. The secret service agent who was engaged on this inquiry discovered, further, that the division was to cruise in northern waters, perhaps even as far as Iceland.

In due course it sailed, and was away for nearly three weeks.

The return of the ships found our agent again in Kiel, and in less than a week he had secured a fairly complete account of the cruise!

Before going ashore the bluejackets from the ships in question had been expressly cautioned by their officers not to talk about the events of the cruise. This was probably a mistake, for experience proves that when a large number of persons are enjoined not to reveal something because it is a strict secret, that 'secret' almost immediately becomes common property.

It was so in this case.

In many a tavern of Kiel the incidents of the cruise were soon being freely discussed by liberty men from the *Elsass* and *Blücher*, some of whom, indeed, talked loudly of the wonderful target practice their ships had made off the Faroe Islands. While information gleaned from tap-room gossip is apt to be misleading, the stories he heard on this occasion tallied so closely as to carry conviction to our man's mind. Once armed with news that, if vague as a whole, was quite definite on certain points, the agent was able to prosecute his inquiry in other quarters. By the sixth day, after a very discreet interview at the 'Franziskaner' café in the Holsten-strasse, he had collected, and verified to his own satisfaction, sufficient material for a long report.

The cruise, it became clear, had been undertaken to test the respective merits of the existing fire-control system, as installed in the *Elsass*, and the new system, with which the *Blücher* was experimentally fitted. A firing ground was chosen some 30 miles south-west of the Faroe Islands, the target being the light cruiser attached to the division. Of course the cruiser herself was not fired at directly. It was what is known in British naval parlance as a 'throw-off' shoot: that is to say, while the gun sights are trained on the target ship, the guns themselves are deflected a fraction out of alignment, with the result that when the aim is true their shots fall some distance astern of her.

The chief advantage of this method – which the Germans claim to have initiated – is that it dispenses with the usual form of gunnery target, which is a heavy and unwieldy structure that can only be towed at rather low speed, and is liable to be wrecked if the weather becomes rough.

The scoring in a throw-off shoot is to some extent approximate, since the conclusive evidence of holes in the target is wanting, but at the same time it is a method that enables the accuracy of gunfire to be determined with a precision sufficient for all practical purposes.

During the first runs on the firing ground the *Elsass* and *Blücher* opened at a range of 11,000 yards, which was gradually increased to 13,000 yards, while the cruiser acting as the target steamed at varying speeds between 14 and 20 knots.

These conditions were abnormally severe for those days, and were, in fact, judged by several British gunnery experts who subsequently 'vetted' the intelligence report to be prohibitive to effective shooting. Yet it is none the less true that some very fine shooting was made on this occasion.

At 11,000 yards, the *Elsass*, with her old type 11-inch guns, was dropping one salvo out of three in the wake of the target, which meant that she would have been hitting frequently but for the slight deflection of her guns. Even at 13,000 yards she had little difficulty in finding and keeping the range.

The *Blücher* was armed with twelve 8.2-inch guns of a new type. She, too, picked up the target with ease, a high percentage of her salvoes pitching in and about the ribbon of broken water that denoted the cruiser's wake.

On the second day the range was extended to 14,000 yards. The weather was clear, and a swell caused the ships to roll slightly. In spite of the increased range, the fire from the *Elsass* was fairly good, but the *Blücher*'s shooting surpassed all expectations.

Steaming at 21 knots, with the target moving at 18, she secured a 'straddle' at the third salvo, and, according to the umpires watching from the target cruiser, one or more hits would certainly have been registered by each of the eleven other broadsides she fired. Having regard to the comparatively small calibre of the guns, the speed at which firing ship and target were travelling, and the state of the sea, the results of this day's shoot were justly considered to be phenomenal.

All these details, and many others, were embodied in the report drafted by the British secret service agent.

When it reached the admiralty certain senior officers were disposed to reject it as spurious. The agent responsible was invited to London to discuss the matter. He was then informed that results such as were recorded in his report were 'absolutely impossible', that no hits could be made on a moving target at any range above 12,000 yards, and that, in short, he had been deceived. This notwithstanding, his own confidence in the accuracy of the figures remained unshaken, and it was with no surprise that he learnt, months later, that his account of the *Blücher-Elsass* cruise had been confirmed in every particular.

By a pure coincidence this development in German naval gunnery took place within a few weeks of the British Navy's first trial of the Scott director system. HMS *Neptune*, the first ship to be fitted with it, carried out experimental practice in March

1911, with excellent results. But official conservatism retarded for nearly a year the extension of the director system to other ships, and it was not until November 1912 that a competitive trial shoot between the *Thunderer*, fitted with director control, and the *Orion*, using the old system, took place. Each ship fired at a separate target, to ensure equal conditions of wind, light, and weather. Sir Percy Scott gave the following description of the practice:

> *The range was 9,000 yards, the ships were steaming at 12 knots speed, and the targets were being towed at the same speed. Immediately the signal was made to open fire, both ships commenced, the* Thunderer *making beautiful shooting and the* Orion *sending her shot all over the place. At the end of three minutes, 'cease fire' was signalled, and an examination of the targets showed that the* Thunderer *had scored six times as many hits as the* Orion.

The interest of this extract lies in the revelation of the difference between British and German gunnery performance at that period. As will be seen, the *Blücher-Elsass* firings were conducted at much greater ranges and speeds than the *Thunderer-Orion* shoot.

To the best of our knowledge, the first British battle practice at 14,000 yards' range was held in 1913, when the *Neptune* scored hits at this distance. Yet only a year or two later our battlecruisers were in action against German ships at a range of over 10 miles, and making very good shooting.

In the Dogger Bank fight, the *Blücher* was disabled by a direct hit at 17,000 yards.

This seems to show that the gunnery experts who scouted

as 'impossible' the results achieved in the German trials off the Faroe Islands had failed to realise what the modern naval gun could do when its fire was controlled by highly scientific methods.

Following the Faroe experiment, the new system of control was applied to all German dreadnoughts and battlecruisers with the least possible delay. Many other practices were held, and of some of these we obtained good reports.

A real triumph was achieved by one of our men in Germany at that time, for he secured actual photographs of certain German targets that had been used for these special gunnery trials.

It is pretty obvious that photographs of that sort would not be hawked about. After all, the German authorities had gone to great expense to obtain confidential information of a very important kind for themselves, and they would watch every print known to be in existence that recorded the results.

They had towed four obsolete battleships out to sea, and these vessels had been simultaneously engaged by the ships of the High Seas Fleet. The photographs that were taken showed the effect on the ships, the damage done to the armour plating, the wreckage occasioned inside the ship, and so on – information of the highest value to those concerned with artillery problems.

Our man got hold of a complete set of the photographs. He never told anyone how he did it, and he died some years ago, so the secret will presumably never be disclosed. But the sensation those photographs caused in the ID will never be forgotten by those who remember their arrival.

Another agent working on naval artillery questions had almost as great a triumph as his colleague who secured the photographs, though in his case it was a matter of piecing together isolated scraps of information rather than the acquirement, complete, of the whole of the documents required.

He put into the hands of the admiralty in the course of a few months full information about the direction-pointer firing system, both for the main and secondary armament of the German ships. He sent through details of the new long-base range-finders, then newly introduced into the capital ships, and other particulars of gunnery equipment. But, more remarkable still, because of the infinitude of detail, he compiled for the admiralty, from fragments of information picked up here and there, complete tabulated statements showing the ballistical qualities of every German naval gun.

He gave the initial velocity, muzzle energy, armour penetration at different ranges, and further details.

His tables differed materially from those passed for publication in technical annuals at the time. It was clear from the evidence he gathered that those tables were simply by way of being catalogues for the information of foreign buyers. They represented the facts about standard models that the German firms were prepared to build for installing in foreign ships (the minor navies nearly all had their ships built in British or German yards in those days), but the figures in the tables were not related very closely to the armament actually produced for the German Navy.

The chief problem of concentrated fire is to distinguish and identify the salvoes from each ship. When two or more ships are engaging the same target, it is soon hidden in a 'forest' of splashes, for the fall of a heavy shell throws up a geyser as high as the masthead, and estimated to contain 2,000 tonnes of water. But unless the splash of each salvo can be instantly identified by the ship that fired it, there is no means of correcting the aim.

This problem was solved by an instrument known in Germany as the '*Aufschlagmelde-Uhr*' (literally, 'splash reporting clock'), and in the British Navy as the 'time-of-flight' clock.

The principle is ingenious but simple. The time taken by a projectile to cover any given distance between the muzzle of the gun and the target being known, the clock is adjusted in accordance with the range at which each salvo is fired. It is set in motion at the instant of discharge, and at the precise moment when the salvo is due to arrive at the target the clock emits a buzzing sound. By this means the gunnery control officer is able to determine which set of splashes comes from his own shots, and so to correct his aim.

But for the time-of-flight clock it would have been impossible for the Germans at Jutland to concentrate so accurate a fire on the *Queen Mary*, which was destroyed by rapid salvoes from the *Derfflinger* and another battlecruiser. In the same way, at a later stage of the action, the *Invincible* was overwhelmed by concentrated fire from the *Lützow* and *Derfflinger*.

As already stated, the German direction-pointer system of control for main and secondary armament, the long-base rangefinders installed in all capital ships of the High Seas Fleet, and many other items of gunnery equipment, were all investigated and reported upon by our secret agents.

Nor was inquiry confined to technical details. We knew, more or less accurately, the gunnery standard of every important German ship; as, for instance, that the *Von der Tann* was at the top of the battlecruiser list for three successive years, that in 1912 the *Posen* was the best-shooting ship of her class, and that the cruisers *Scharnhorst* and *Gneisenau*, of the Asiatic Squadron, were the 'crack' gunnery ships of the whole navy – a fact that received tragic confirmation at the Battle of Coronel, when, in spite of failing light and a rough sea, they covered the *Good Hope* and the *Monmouth* with bursting shell and destroyed both ships with appalling swiftness.

Thus, during the last few years before the war, the guns of the rival fleets facing one another across the grey North Sea were steadily thundering away in preparation for the supreme test of battle, when the lath-and-canvas targets of peacetime would be replaced by great, steel-clad ships housing hundreds of men – targets that not only hit back at their assailants, but sometimes returned the fire with terrible effect.

Amidst the tumult and smoke of battle, with ships moving at utmost speed and turning this way and that to confuse the enemy's aim, it would be too much to expect the same degree of accuracy in shooting as can be attained under the less disturbing conditions of ordinary target practice. Those who had observed the development of German naval gunnery before the war knew what we had to expect, and if they were surprised at all, it was only by the fact that in the Battle of Jutland the German percentage of hits to rounds fired did not exceed three and a half.

CHAPTER 9

PROBING DOCKYARD SECRETS

ELSEWHERE IN THIS book allusion is made to the frequent and severe epidemics of 'spionitis', or spy fever, that ravaged Germany in pre-war days. There is no doubt that the bacilli were cultivated and sowed broadcast by the government, which found these recurrent espionage scares very beneficial to their grandiose naval plans. The newspapers, with a few honourable exceptions, did their utmost to create the impression that Germany swarmed with foreign spies, the majority of whom were working for England; yet, as we have seen, the actual number of British agents regularly doing naval intelligence work in Europe was very small. They could have been enumerated on one hand, leaving a finger or two to spare at that. These men must not be confused with the amateurs – both officers on leave and civilians – who tried to pick up naval and military information on their visits to Germany.

It is a noteworthy fact that not one of our permanent intelligence men was ever caught by the German authorities in peacetime. One or two of them had narrow escapes, as we shall see; but in no case could sufficient evidence be gathered to justify an arrest. This circumstance speaks volumes for the discretion with which they carried out their duty. Although infinitely more circumspect than the German emissaries operating in England, they nevertheless garnered ten times as much information of real value. The comparative immunity they enjoyed reflects no small credit on the methods of the British secret service as a whole.

Incredible as it may sound, the life was often monotonous, and even boring. An agent might spend days or weeks following up a promising clue that eventually turned out to be worthless; or, having picked up in an hour some item of news that seemed of vital importance, it might take him a month of travelling and tedious investigation to verify it, for mere rumours or doubtful information were not welcomed at ID headquarters. Only facts were wanted there, facts that would bear the test of expert scrutiny.

In this, as in every other profession, the zealous beginner was apt to take his calling too seriously.

Unless of very exceptional calibre, he spent the first few months discovering mares' nests, traversing ground of which his predecessors had explored every inch, and filling the capacious waste-paper baskets at headquarters with reports that would have been obsolete a year back. But this phase soon passed, and with it any incipient temptation to emulate the stage effects of the 'shilling-shocker' sleuth.

There was no scope for histrionics. Disguises were sometimes worn, but only as an extreme measure. The one indispensable piece of camouflage was a legitimate occupation that could be made to account for every overt form of activity that the real work in hand might entail.

In addition to the technical knowledge that was a *sine qua non*, a command of the language of the country was essential. The best agents were of necessity good social 'mixers', for this quality enabled them to mingle freely with all sorts and conditions of people, and thus gave them many opportunities of picking up news that they would otherwise have missed.

Steady nerves were, of course, a great asset, for the secret service man was liable at any moment to find himself in an awkward situation that demanded perfect coolness and presence of mind if the coils were not to close round him. Yet the very nature of the work imposed a constant strain on the nervous system. One of the best men we had in Germany suffered badly from neurasthenia, but still contrived to carry on and, indeed, to perform several daring exploits while his malady was at its height. He found excitement an excellent palliative while it lasted, though the reaction was always severe.

Secret service is a popular theme with writers of fiction, but since none of these appears to have had personal experience of the subject, their impressions are more diverting than instructive. We have been fortunate in persuading a former member of the service to give us, in outline, an account of his work in central Europe over a period of about six months. This we believe to be the first authentic narrative of its kind ever published. Our informant, it should be added, was in quest of naval intelligence only. Actual dates are omitted, but the year was 1912. We present the story in his own words.

On returning from London to my pied à terre *in Germany, I spent some days on paper work, and then proceeded to Danzig, which had not been visited for some time.*

Information was wanted about the battleship König Albert, *building at the Schichau yard, and the battlecruiser* Ersatz Kaiserin Augusta *(Lützow), on the stocks at the same yard; the submarines in hand at the government dockyard, and seaplane trials at the Putzig naval aerodrome.*

It was cold as only Danzig can be. I put up at the 'Reichshof', and spent the first day in paying one or two genuine business calls, being careful to let the desk people know where I was going.

On the second day the usual batch of mail arrived for me. This further established my respectability with the hotel people and, of course, with the police, who in every German seaport were known, at that time, to take a special interest in English visitors.

A word of explanation about this 'usual batch of mail'. I made it a practice, before paying a professional visit to any city, to arrange for the forwarding of certain letters that both outwardly and inwardly confirmed the ostensible purpose of my visit. If those letters were intercepted or otherwise tampered with, their effect would be to dispel any suspicions that may have been harboured by the authorities. It was a very simple precaution, but I always found it effective.

To gain access to the Schichau yard was easy enough. I went in with Jacobs, a Pole, whom I knew to be trustworthy. He was an electrical fitter, and was then working on board a cargo steamer that had been built by the firm. I was able to make a close inspection of the König Albert. *She had her guns in position, but was less advanced than we had believed.*

The battlecruiser was on the main building-slip, having been laid down in the previous autumn. She had been reported to us as being almost a replica of the Derfflinger – *of which we had pretty full details – and her appearance, although the hull had not been entirely plated up, confirmed this.*

Altogether I spent three hours in the yard. The risk of detection was small. At that time the shipyard staff numbered nearly 3,000, as a large amount of work, both naval and mercantile, was in progress.

I did not notice any special precautions against unauthorised sightseeing. Every workman was supposed to show a card on entering the gates, but nine-tenths of them ignored this formality.

Access to the government dockyard was more difficult. Situated north of the city on the western bank of the Vistula, it is rather isolated. There is a ferry service between the dockyard and the 'Kaiser-hafen' on the opposite bank, but I thought it unsafe to use this. A general view of the yard could be obtained from the little steamers that run between Danzig and Neufahrwasser, but the submarines, which I particularly wanted to see, were built on covered slipways roofed with glass.

Eventually I did get in, and had a good look at four submarines on the stocks and two that were in the fitting-out basin; but it was exceedingly risky, and I cut the visit as short as possible.

The facts I memorised on this occasion cleared up a number of points on which our people had been doubtful. Some confusion as to the actual number of boats completed and building at any given date was caused by the practice of sending to Danzig dockyard, to receive confidential items of equipment, boats that had been built and engined at the Krupp-Germania yard in Kiel. Conversely, Danzig-built submarines were sometimes sent to the Germania yard for machinery overhaul. But from January 1913 we had a system by which the number of ready and building submarines could be checked once a month.

I next went to Zoppot, a pleasant bathing-beach north of Danzig. On the outskirts of this place was the Putzig naval flying station. I saw six seaplanes exercising, and made notes on the hangars, shops, and oil tanks. By this time I had been long enough in the district, and judged it advisable to cancel an intended visit to Elbing, where the Schichau firm had another big yard that specialised in destroyer construction. So I returned to Berlin and spent a couple of days in collating my notes and writing reports. The memorandum on the submarines was much appreciated at headquarters.

A special journey to Munich, to meet a man – a Czech – who was employed at the big Skoda plant in Pilsen (Bohemia), which made all the guns and armour for the Austrian Navy. This man had been named to me as a likely correspondent. Our negotiation was satisfactory, and I provisionally engaged him. He turned out to be a treasure, for besides sending in good reports himself, he put me into touch with a friend at Pola who was very useful when I visited that Austrian naval base.

From Munich I went to Düsseldorf. The attraction here were the Ehrhardt gun shops, which were building 3.4-inch and 4.1-inch guns for new cruisers, besides some experimental light guns for submarines.

There were absolutely no precautions here, and I not only visited the shops, but also obtained some exact details of the work – partly from the workmen's bench cards, and partly by other means.

From Düsseldorf to Essen. Here I had a bad disappointment, for a correspondent whom I had deemed reliable failed to turn up at the rendezvous. He had promised to accompany me to the Krupp shops where the new 12-inch fifty-calibre guns were being machined. After waiting an hour, I thought it best to leave Essen at once, as his absence was suspicious. I never heard from this man again, but as there were no unpleasant developments, it was probably a case of 'cold feet'. However, I avoided Essen for several months after that.

As the weather was now warmer, I went to the neighbourhood of Kiel. Stayed there a fortnight, but not in the town itself. Visited the Howaldt and Krupp-Germania yards, getting a glimpse of new submarines at the latter, but found the government yard too closely guarded.

This trip was undertaken mainly with the object of securing submarine data, and in this respect it was most successful. I found a delightful spot a few miles north-west of the entrance to Kiel harbour, where the U-boats came out to do diving practice. Several days were profitably spent here.

I discovered, among other things, that the German boats were sluggish in diving compared with ours, and took nearly a minute longer to submerge. The boats appeared to be handled with extreme caution, probably due to the scare that had been caused by the sinking of U-3 in January 1911. It was clear that submarine training was being conducted on 'safety first' principles.

The Kiel visit provided material for a very long report.

My next journey was to the North Sea coast. I saw the battleship Grosser Kurfürst at the Vulkan yard at Hamburg, and inspected a sister ship, the Markgraf, on the stocks at the Weser yard in Bremen. These inspections, I may add, always revealed interesting points, but they would not interest non-technical readers.

At the Blohm and Voss yard in Hamburg a very thorough survey was made of the battlecruiser Derfflinger, the first of the 12-inch gun type.

Passing this yard in one of the excursion steamers that do the

'Hafen-Rundfahrt' *trip, I had a mildly humorous interlude. Our guide was a large, pompous person who declaimed in a loud voice on the marvels we were witnessing. When the* Derfflinger *came into view I pointed at her, and innocently asked 'whether it was a torpedo boat'.*

The guide nearly had apoplexy:

'Ein Torpedo-boot! Herr Gott! *Why, that's a battlecruiser, the largest in the world!'*

He was so appalled at my ignorance that from then on he insisted on giving me details of every ship we saw. Unfortunately, they were all wrong. But I did not enlighten him.

An excursion from Hamburg to Cuxhaven resulted in material for a good report on the local minesweeping flotillas. The battle-cruiser Von der Tann *was anchored off the port, and I determined to visit her, though the risk was considerable.*

By a stroke of luck I found that a local shipping man, to whom I had a letter from a mutual friend in Berlin, knew several officers of the ship, and had visited them on board. He was going again, and by very tactful manoeuvring I got him to invite me to accompany him. We went across in a launch, but on arriving at the ship's ladder I remarked to my companion that, being a foreigner, I might not be welcome on board. He then spoke to the officer of the watch, who was one of his friends, explained who I was (or, more strictly speaking, who he thought I was), and I was promptly invited to come up. We spent two hours in the ship, and saw nearly everything except the inside of the gun turrets and the engine room.

Judged by British standards she was terribly cramped. The mess decks were low, stuffy, and overcrowded. Lieutenants and junior officers berthed four to the cabin. Every piece of furniture in the ship was made of metal. It was easy to see that she was very strongly built. Each of the 6-inch guns was completely isolated, and could only be knocked out by a direct hit. I memorised all the important details, and subsequently wrote an elaborate report on the ship. This was the first German battlecruiser to be personally inspected by a British secret service man.

From Cuxhaven I went to Heligoland, then back to Berlin to meet two correspondents who brought 'highly important' news. On examination I found that we had known it six months before.

My next journey was to Vienna, where I wished to make certain contacts before beginning a tour of the Austro-Hungarian bases. Called at the headquarters of the Austrian Navy League, and was not surprised to find the principal organiser a German.

Then to Trieste, to look at the battleships building at the Stabilimento Tecnico. Here there were no precautions whatever, and I spent two days in the yard.

From Trieste to Pola, the chief naval harbour. Here things were run more on Prussian lines: sentries all over the place and dockyard strictly guarded. Admiral Anton Haus, the Minister of Marine, was convinced that there were two hundred Italian spies in Pola. I met a correspondent of strong Italian sympathies. He was a shipwright, and gave me a mass of information about the four Austrian dreadnoughts, Viribus Unitis *class. According to him, they were of inferior design and deficient in stability; moreover, the workmanship put into them was bad. I was inclined to doubt this at the time, but it may well have been true, for in the last year of the war the* Szent Istvan *of this class foundered after being hit by one small torpedo.*

I got some interesting impressions of the Austro-Hungarian naval personnel. The bluejackets were a heterogeneous crowd, speaking half a dozen tongues or dialects, Italian predominating.

They did not make a good appearance, and were lacking in discipline. The absence of esprit de corps *could almost be felt.*

The officers were more like military men than sailors – very arrogant towards their men. I did not need to be told that cases of insubordination on the lower deck were very frequent. After observing these conditions at first-hand, I was not surprised when the Kaiserliche und Königliche Kriegsmarine *soon began to crack under the strain of war. On the other hand, many of the officers were fine fellows, Admiral Horthy, in particular, being a leader of whom any country might be proud.*

This trip was extended down the Dalmatian coast to Cattaro, where the fortifications were inspected. This was the base from which, during the war, the Austrian cruisers raided the Otranto barrage. It was also the headquarters of German U-boats working in the Mediterranean.

Back to Vienna and Berlin, and thence to England on a fortnight's leave. The rural peace of the West Country was a much-needed sedative for frayed nerves.

Broke the return journey at London for a conference, at which I received further instructions.

Kept an appointment in Berlin, and then proceeded to Kiel, for inquiries into submarine engines and other matters.

Then to North Sea coast again for a tour of the islands – Sylt, Heligoland, Wangerooge, Norderney, and Borkum. The incidents of this trip would make a story in themselves. As it was undertaken at a time when Germany was in the throes of spy fever, and the islands in question were considered to be of great military importance – 'the fatherland's natural rampart against English attack', as the German Navy League phrased it – the utmost care was necessary to avoid suspicion.

In the foregoing brief account of six months' work I have said nothing about thrilling episodes. But from time to time they did occur.

On one of my trips to Berlin I kept an appointment with a correspondent who had previously given me a considerable amount of useful information. Although German by nationality, he had a Polish mother. He was highly intelligent, but most excitable, and I had always foreseen trouble with him.

On this occasion he came to the meeting place in a state of extreme nervous tension. The police were on his track, he assured me, and he had been shadowed for several days. He also believed that his correspondence was being opened. He lived in fear of arrest at any moment. He could not sleep, and he was drinking too much. So he had made up his mind to go to the police and confess.

By implicating me he expected to get off lightly, as he knew the authorities would consider me a valuable catch. It was something in his favour that he had come to warn me of what he proposed to do. Had he gone to the police first I should have been caught red-handed, for they would naturally have instructed him to pass incriminating documents to me before they came to make the arrest.

Even as things were, it was an awkward situation. Schneider, as I will call him, was in that condition of extreme fear that makes the veriest poltroon take desperate risks if he sees the faintest chance of saving his skin. I argued with him for a long time, assuring him that his fears were baseless, and pointing out that even confession would not save him from a stiff term of imprisonment. But it was all in vain. He was going straight to the police, and no one should stop him.

That did not suit me at all. If he persisted in his intention, I must at least have time to get clear of Berlin, and once the police were on the alert this would be difficult, if not impossible.

It was clearly a case for drastic methods. Schneider made for the door, but I reached it first, locked it, and put the key in my pocket. He struggled with me, and I had to hit him – hard. I did this reluctantly, for until then he had been exceedingly useful to me, and in any case I did not want to make him a personal enemy.

He collapsed in a chair. I gave him a drink and then produced a revolver, just for moral effect. Then I talked to him.

It's amazing how fertile one's imagination becomes in a crisis like this. I painted a lurid picture of our secret service, of its ramifications all over the world, and of the ruthless treatment it meted out to betrayers. Its agents worked in couples, I said, though only one actually operated at a time; the other remained in the background, ready to execute swift vengeance if his colleague came to harm.

'You tell me you've been shadowed these last few days, Schneider,' I said. 'Well, that happens to be true. But it wasn't by the police. You have been kept under close observation by my colleague. We always shadow people like you as a matter of routine. It is extremely fortunate for you that you did not attempt to go to the police before seeing me again. Had you attempted to do so you would have been a dead man by now. On leaving this house you will again be followed, and I advise you to go straight home. Otherwise something will happen to you.'

He was inclined to be sceptical at first; but although I was bluffing, the knowledge of my own danger made me feel, and probably look, rather grim. Gradually I could see conviction dawning in his eyes. And this much was true enough: that I was not going to let him out of my sight until I was reasonably sure that his lips were sealed.

Finally he said that he would not make his confession till the following morning, so that I would have the whole night in which to escape. But I saw through this stratagem, for it was obvious that, unless he could produce me, his story would merely convict himself without securing lenient treatment from the authorities. It was necessary to use more powerful arguments.

I warned him that betrayal of me at any time would infallibly be punished.

'If the police allow you to go free, it will only be a question of days, perhaps hours, before something very unpleasant happens to you. If you get a prison sentence, no matter how long it may be, my friends will be waiting for you when you are released. Go where you will, you cannot escape them!'

Then I tried a further bluff.

'And here's another thing, my friend. Hasn't it occurred to you that you are more at my mercy than I am at yours? Now that you have shown yourself to be untrustworthy, I am half inclined to give you a dose of your own medicine. I am going to summon one of my colleagues' (turning to the telephone as I spoke) 'who will see that you are kept quiet for the next day or two, by which time I shall be out of Germany. You will then be anonymously denounced to the police as a spy, and conclusive evidence of your guilt will be placed in their hands. If you try to implicate me you probably won't be believed, and in any case it won't help you. You will be safe for ten years, and, as you know, the prison people have orders to make things specially severe for men convicted of Landesverrat. Yes, that is by far the best plan.' And I made as if to lift the telephone receiver.

The bluff had undoubtedly worked. Schneider was now in a more pitiable state of terror than before. He saw that my threat could really be put into execution, and he capitulated without further ado. He swore that he would not go to the police, promised to do anything I told him, and, as evidence of good faith, there and then produced some information that was really valuable.

But still I was not satisfied. In his present state of agitation he was not to be trusted. So I determined to keep him with me all night, hoping that by morning he would have recovered his nerve. It was a long and trying night, and more than once I had to make play with the revolver to keep him quiet.

After certain forms of moral suasion had been employed, he drew up, in his own handwriting, a full confession of the work he had done for me – giving dates and all details – and signed it. This I put into an envelope and addressed it to the Chief of Police, Berlin.

'Now, Schneider,' I said, 'if in the future I have any reason to doubt you, this envelope goes into the post at once. You must see that there's no escape if you ever attempt to give me away.'

He obviously did see it, and I began to feel more confident. In the morning I called a taxi and drove him to his rooms in Charlottenburg. He was pretty much of a wreck by then, but the nervous crisis was over, and he was quite subdued. I had paid him off, and privately decided not to employ him again. I had also settled my bill at the hotel and brought my bag away. As Schneider was getting out of the cab I told the driver to go to the Friedrichstrasse station, but when we had covered a short distance I re-directed him to the Anhalter, as I was going south.

After a wearisome cross-country journey, broken at several points to make sure I was not being followed, I got to my headquarters late at night. Although Schneider had not known this address, I deemed it wise to move elsewhere. As weeks passed and nothing happened, it became evident that he was holding his tongue. I never saw or heard of him again.

It was always a risky business dealing with such people, for a man who will sell his own country will, as a rule, make nothing of selling those for whom he works. Yet, strangely enough, none of the men whom I employed ever gave me away, though several threatened to do so. No doubt they knew that even turning Kaiser's evidence would not save them from a sharp sentence.

You ask, 'What about the agent provocateur?' Well, I came across three or four members of that tribe, and can only say that they would not have deceived an intelligent infant. They almost invariably gave themselves away at the first interview.

Only one ever proved troublesome – a certain Konrad Schumacher, or so he called himself. He was instrumental in causing the arrest of an agent who was working on behalf of a certain government – not the British. This agent had done splendid work, but he must have been simple to have walked into the trap that Schumacher laid.

Shortly afterwards I myself came into contact with the wily Konrad, and passed on some information about him to a friend, who was connected with the government in question. In due course a snare was set. Schumacher was lured across the frontier to meet a high foreign officer who proposed to do a little intelligence work in Germany, and was anxious to have the agent provocateur's assistance, for which he offered a tempting bribe. But the visit was never made. When Schumacher arrived at the rendezvous he was promptly arrested as a German spy, and on being searched he was found to be in possession of some most incriminating documents.

He swore by all the Teutonic deities that he had never seen them *before. In that case one wonders how they found their way into his pocket! His protestations did not save him, and he got six years' rigorous imprisonment. In dealing with one of his kidney you cannot afford to observe Queensberry rules.*

CHAPTER 10

UNRIDDLING THE SANDS

THE IMPERIAL GERMAN Navy possessed twenty-four fortified bases, stations, and depots in its home waters. Nine were situated on the North Sea coast and thirteen in the Baltic, while the remaining two were inland – Neumünster, in Holstein, being the naval wireless headquarters, and Dietrichsdorf, near Kiel, the principal ammunition magazine for the fleet.

By many critics the number of bases was deemed excessive. Not only were they costly to maintain, since most of them had elaborate defences manned by *Matrosen-Artillerie*, i.e. seamen-gunners, but it was feared that they might exert an enervating influence on the fleet in time of war. For the same reason the Spartans disliked walled cities.

When a commander is conscious of having a safe line of retreat he will be less inclined to fight to a finish. History teems with examples of this, and the Great War contributed not a few. There is little doubt that the German fleet would have accomplished much more than it did had there been fewer defended positions to which it could retire when hard pressed. On the other hand, we must not forget that as the German Navy was originally conceived as a coast-defence force, its first battleships – Siegfried class, laid down in 1888–92 – having been built expressly for the protection of the Kiel Canal, there was a traditional tendency to exaggerate the value of brick-and-mortar defences as a naval asset.

For obvious reasons, the British secret service was chiefly interested in the German North Sea coastline. It stretches some 220 miles from the Ems estuary to the Danish frontier. Shoals and sandbanks make it difficult of approach, and thus form a natural defence. Even under ordinary conditions navigation in these waters is difficult and hazardous. In wartime, with coastwise lights extinguished and channel buoys removed, the most skilful pilot would hesitate to trust himself within this labyrinth of shifting sand. To ships of deep draught it is inaccessible save by certain channels in which the dredgers have to be kept continuously at work. When to these natural barriers were added minefields and powerful batteries, the German western littoral became an impregnable rampart against which the mightiest fleet would have spent its strength in vain.

In the light of a fact so manifest it is strange that the Germans were unable to rid themselves of the nightmare of a British naval assault on their coast. It was partly this obsession that paralysed the High Seas Fleet during the early months of the war and left the British Navy in undisputed command of the sea at a period when the mere hint of a challenge to its supremacy would have caused the Allies grave embarrassment.

There was, however, this much excuse for the caution, which the German Navy carried to extreme lengths: a descent upon one or more of the German offshore islands and their seizure as advanced bases for operations against the mainland did actually form part of the British plan of war strategy, though it was ultimately decided to abandon the project. The secret, such as it is, has already been revealed by Mr Winston Churchill in his second volume of *The World Crisis*.

Borkum was chosen as the principal objective because it was furthest from the great naval base of Wilhelmshaven, and might thus be successfully attacked before a relieving force had time to arrive. With Borkum in our hands it might have been feasible to land troops at Emden, and, if not to thrust an invading army into Western Prussia, at any rate to create a diversion that must have seriously disorganised German military strategy. The naval expedition against Borkum was to have been led by Admiral Sir Lewis Bayly. Unfortunately the sinking of HMS *Formidable* by a German submarine, while that battleship was attached to his command, momentarily clouded his reputation, and for this and other reasons the plan was shelved.

Perhaps it was as well, for the venture would have been a desperate one. That Borkum might have been seized by a bold *coup de main* is likely enough; but that it could long have been held against the violent counter-attacks that the Germans would certainly have launched without delay is exceedingly doubtful. The outstanding merit of the plan was that its execution would, in all probability, have speedily brought about a great fleet action, ante-dating Jutland by more than twelve months, and possibly fought in circumstances more advantageous to the British fleet.

It will readily be understood, therefore, that our naval intelligence department was anxious to learn all about Borkum and its defences. And despite the redoubled vigilance of the Germans after the Brandon–Trench affair, the information desired was duly forthcoming.

Contrary to widespread belief, we were not particularly interested in Heligoland. It is true there were optimists at the admiralty who believed that we could conquer and hold this island, which would, it was assumed, give us virtual command of the German Bight itself; but the navy as a whole regarded the plan as impracticable, and shortly after the outbreak of war it was rejected by Admiral Jellicoe after a conference with the admiralty chiefs. But since it is wise to prepare for every contingency, our pre-war secret service by no means ignored Heligoland. It was, in fact, pretty thoroughly surveyed, and held no surprise for us.

The insignificant island of Wangerooge was considered to be much more important, for it lies only 20 miles north of Wilhelmshaven, the High Seas Fleet's war base. Long-range guns firing from these wind-whipped sand dunes would completely dominate the fairway leading from the great naval port, thus bottling up the fleet inside.

The Germans were slow in apprehending this danger, for it was not until 1910 that they began to fortify Wangerooge. Then, however, they made a thorough job of it.

Another place in which we were interested was Sylt, Germany's northernmost island in the North Sea.

It would be possible to fill this chapter with complete and minute details of every German naval base and sea fortress that existed in 1914, all supplied by our intelligence agents before that date. Needless to say, the collection of this mass of data involved a great deal of hard work and personal risk, but today its interest is mainly historical. But some of the methods by which it was obtained deserve to be indicated. As told in an earlier page, reliable maps of Borkum showing the position and strength of the defences were in possession of the British Admiralty three years before the war. Here is the story by the man who provided them:

After the very gallant exploits of Brandon and Trench in 1910, the Germans kept a much keener watch all round the coast, and every foreigner became suspect. At every large port the local police were reinforced by detectives who had received special training in counter-espionage work. These men did their best, no doubt, but they had very little success, beyond rounding up dozens of quite harmless people. In one month they arrested four persons at Heligoland, three at Kiel, and two at Indem, all of whom proved to be entirely innocent of espionage.

The first important mission I undertook was an investigation of the defences of Emden and Borkum.

Emden had only recently come into prominence as a naval base, though we had always regarded it as one of the potential jumping-off points of a German invasion of England. In 1910 our attention was attracted by the extensive harbour works that had been started there, the scale of which seemed out of proportion to the ordinary shipping requirements of the port. The channel, 2.5 miles in length, which leads from the estuary up to Emden, was deepened sufficiently to take vessels drawing 30 feet of water. Adjacent to the harbour itself a huge basin was excavated, large enough to contain a fleet of big ships. The wharf frontage was equipped with up-to-date gear for handling heavy weights, and between Emden town station and the new basin there were quadruple railway tracks.

Several hundred acres of reclaimed land westward of the town had been purchased by the state, and at the time of my visit large barracks and other military buildings were being erected there. The small local shipbuilding yard, Nordsee-Werke, had just been bought by a syndicate in which Krupps held the controlling interest. It was being enlarged and equipped with new plant, and the management announced that it would soon be in a position to build or repair ships of any dimensions.

This activity at Emden was so pronounced that suspicion was aroused in England. No conviction was carried by semi-official articles in the German press, explaining that Emden's assured future as a great commercial entrepôt necessitated the provision of adequate port facilities. On the contrary, everything indicated that Emden was being developed as a base for oversea military operations. It was admirably situated for this purpose. Screened from observation by the chain of Frisian islands, it would have been possible to assemble a fleet of transports in the Ems with absolute secrecy, while the excellent railway communications between the port and military depôts inland would enable large bodies of troops to be concentrated and embarked with great rapidity.

Delfzyl, a Dutch town on the other side of the Ems, had been suggested to me as a convenient base for intelligence work in the Emden district; but having heard that the German authorities kept an eye on foreigners coming from the Dutch side, I determined to make my headquarters at Leer, some 15 miles distant from Emden. As the morning and evening trains between these places were always crowded, there was very little risk of becoming conspicuous.

But to make assurance doubly sure I was careful to wear

German-made clothes. This was a simple but effective disguise, as all who are acquainted – for their sins – with German 'reach-me-downs' will readily understand.

I did not carry a notebook or any documents other than those that purported to reveal my identity, for I rigidly abstained from making notes under any circumstances when engaged in this sort of work. With a little practice it is easy to memorise quite copious details, so long as one is familiar with the technicalities of the subject and knows what to look for.

I had timed my visit to coincide with a 'surprise mobilisation' of the Borkum-Emden defences, hints of which had been allowed to appear in the Hamburg papers. These exercises were held about twice a year, their object being to determine how soon it was possible to land powerful reinforcements for the Borkum garrison.

Incidentally the experience gained on one such occasion in midwinter, when ice in the Ems held up the transports, resulted in a decision so to strengthen the garrison of Borkum as to render it more or less independent of aid from the mainland.

The widespread publicity given to certain phases of German naval and military manoeuvres – in striking contrast to the absolute secrecy observed as a general rule – may have puzzled some people, but it was easily explained. When the government wanted money for fortifying some point on the coast, they staged a sham attack that, of course, met with complete success. The newspapers then came out with scare articles expatiating on the defenceless state of the 'vital' point in question, and the temptation it offered to a would-be invader – these articles being sent out from the press department of the German Admiralty. 'Public opinion' having been mobilised in this way, the Reichstag usually voted the requisite funds for building new coastal defences.

I reached Emden a few hours before the troop trains began to arrive. They came from Munster, headquarters of the 7th Army Corps, and brought about four battalions of infantry, a few companies of engineers, and four batteries of field artillery, with several machine-gun detachments.

The trains passed over the new tracks leading down to the harbour and ran alongside the three steamers berthed there. So quickly were the troops and batteries embarked that all three ships were able to cast off in less than an hour.

The voyage to Borkum was accomplished in two hours, and the disembarkation took just seventy-five minutes.

Thus, from the arrival of the trains at Emden to the landing of the last man and gun at Borkum hardly more than four hours had elapsed. It was a smart piece of work, and the clockwork precision with which everything had been carried out spoke well for the staff organisation.

The whole operation was conducted quite openly. Crowds watched the troops embark at Emden, and, when the transports sailed, an excursion steamer followed in their wake, lying off the island while the landing was in progress. From this steamer I was able to watch the entire proceedings. The excursionists got ashore soon afterwards.

With other people I walked among the troops while they were having their dinner from the Goulasch-Kanonen, *as they called the field kitchens. To them the whole thing was a picnic.*

I approached quite close to one of the batteries, the entrance to which was guarded with barbed wire. The solitary sentry was at the far end of his beat, chatting to visitors, and it would have been perfectly easy to enter the battery. But I should probably have been seen by other people, and therefore judged the risk to be not worthwhile.

I noted the position of the battery, made other observations, and then strolled along the sea wall that runs parallel with the railway to its terminus at Victoriahöhe, near the lifeboat station. On the way I passed two more batteries, getting a good view of the second, which contained four howitzers with revolving armoured cupolas.

There were several sentries about, but they took no notice of the harmless citizen from Emden who was giving his new summer suit – price 50 marks! – an airing in the sea breeze.

I saw the field guns being railed from the landing stage to the sea front. Two collapsible observation towers for artillery control had been brought from the mainland, and these were erected and manned. In rear of the second coast battery was an armoured fire-control station with a very large range-finder; the base I estimated at 25 feet.

Here I may interpolate that the calibre of the guns in the batteries was ascertained, not by a direct inspection of the guns, but by observing ammunition being unloaded from railway trucks at Emden for shipment to the island. Howitzer shells of 11 inches and gun projectiles of 9.4 inches were definitely identified.

I noticed at Borkum that all along the railway there was a high embankment that made the line invisible from the sea, and that this embankment was so skilfully buttressed with sanded concrete that, at a distance, it must have been indistinguishable from the sand dunes, the more so as the parapet was undulated to conform roughly with the contour of the dunes. The battery and observation positions were camouflaged in the same way. As I subsequently found by cruising round the island in an excursion steamer, these positions could not be made out even at a short distance offshore, so perfectly did they merge with the sandhills. I was convinced that no naval bombardment could be relied upon to reduce the defences, seeing that the targets were invisible and could only be hit by chance shots. This, of course, was before the days of aircraft 'spotting'.

The return journey to Emden, and thence to Leer, was made without incident.

A few days later I went to Norddeich and viewed the naval wireless station with its six tall masts. From there I crossed to the island of Norderney, which, according to reports we had received, was then being fortified. I spent two days at the Deutsches Haus, walked practically all over the island, and satisfied myself beyond doubt that there was not a single gun in the place. Nor was there any garrison. The island, in fact, remained unfortified until just before the outbreak of war.

Wangerooge was my next objective. Beyond the fact that it had recently been provided with strong defences, we had very little information about this island. It was my business to make good this deficiency, but the task had to be approached with great discretion; first, because Wangerooge now ranked as a key position in the scheme of coastal defence, and was therefore closely guarded; and, secondly, because it was difficult of access. Hamburg–Amerika and Norddeutscher Lloyd excursion steamers, from Cuxhaven and Bremerhaven respectively, called there during the bathing season; but on the day of my visit the only means of reaching the island was by a tiny steamship from Harle, an obscure village on the Norden-Sande coast railway.

This line traverses country with which all readers of The Riddle of the Sands will be familiar, passing through such places as Esens, Jever, and Carolinensiel, where Davies and Carruthers, of the Dulcibella, had divers adventures.

There was no great traffic along this line, and all the regular passengers were known to the railway officials. Strangers were *therefore apt to attract attention, and the presence of an obvious foreigner – especially an Englishman – would certainly have been commented upon, and in all probability reported to the police. Clearly, therefore, it would be safer to go in the guise of a German tripper, and this I did. It was one of the very few occasions on which I adopted a disguise more elaborate than a German ready-made suit of clothes.*

It is a dreary journey to Harle. The train runs through flat, depressing country, dotted here and there with insignificant hamlets and church spires. The prevailing tone is grey – grey landscape, grey skies, and occasional glimpses of the grey North Sea, fringed with sand dunes and grey mud flats.

From Harle the little steamer makes the trip to Wangerooge under an hour. Including myself, there were only a dozen passengers on board. In order to discourage the sociable overtures of my fellow passengers I spent the time in consuming one of those Gargantuan lunches, put up in numerous paper bags, without which no self-respecting German tripper would in those days have dreamed of starting on his travels.

On the little landing stage at Wangerooge there were two policemen and several bluejackets, the latter having Matrosenartillerie *cap ribbons that showed them to belong to the naval coast artillery corps. The police officers scrutinised us rather closely, but no one was interrogated. Lying alongside the pier were a naval tug and two lighters, marked 'Königlich Marinewerft (royal dockyard), Wilhelmshaven'.*

A narrow-gauge railway runs from the pier to the village. I had a meal at the Kurhaus Hotel, bathed, and then sat in a beach café over a glass of beer for an hour. It would not have done to start a tour of the island immediately after landing. In due course I began my exploration. There were several parties of pedestrians, and I kept near one of these, as though I were a straggler.

The battery positions were easily discovered, each zone being shut off by palisades and barbed wire, the entrance guarded by a sentry. The principal battery appeared to be that situated near the old church tower to the west of the village, this part of the shore being protected by groynes from the fierce North Sea breakers. Access to the battery was impossible, but from various indications I judged it to contain four 9.4-inch guns.

Two similar guns were emplaced in another battery to the east of the village, while still further in that direction workmen were engaged on what was obviously to be a new battery. This was subsequently armed with two 11-inch guns. I memorised the position of each battery and such details of its lay-out as were to be seen. Behind the new battery very deep excavations were in progress, obviously for the magazines.

Here, as at Borkum, the defences were so arranged and camouflaged as to be practically invisible from the sea, and the prospect of reducing them by naval bombardment appeared to be poor.

I spent that night on the island, intending to resume my survey on the following day; but in the morning something occurred that upset my plans. In the hall of the Kurhaus Hotel I noticed a man studying the register. There was that in his appearance that suggested the plain-clothes policeman. Afterwards he engaged in conversation with the reception clerk, with whom I had exchanged a few words that morning.

I felt no particular uneasiness at this moment, and walked down to the beach. Halfway there I turned, and saw the plain-clothes man 100 yards behind me. He might or might not be following me, but I was taking no chances. Instead of continuing my walk along the shore I sat down and smoked a cigar. The detective promptly sat down too, still keeping the same distance from me. An hour passed; I rose, and sauntered in the direction of the church tower, only to find the man on my tracks again. There was no longer room for doubt; I was being shadowed.

In these circumstances there was but one thing to do – leave the island as quickly as possible, if it were not too late. True, there was no evidence that I had been engaged in espionage, since I had not entered any of the batteries or taken notes or photographs; but I was carrying identity papers that would not bear too minute a scrutiny. If these were found to be irregular, that fact, coupled with my presence in a fortified zone, would be quite sufficient to ensure my being detained, pending further inquiries; and if my movements during the previous fortnight were traced – as probably they would be – the authorities would have convincing, if only circumstantial, evidence of what my activities connoted.

The position looked critical, and I set my wits to work. If I attempted to leave the island while the detective remained suspicious he would probably detain me, in which event I should certainly be taken to the mainland to face a searching examination by higher police officials. On the other hand, to remain at Wangerooge would be purposeless. The third alternative was to attempt a bluff, which, if it failed, would leave me in no worse case than before. So I retraced my steps to the village, made for the nearest café, and ordered a beer. In a few moments my faithful shadow appeared, took his seat a few tables away, and ordered a similar refreshment. The time had come to try my bluff.

Glass of beer in hand, I crossed over to the detective's table, and, with a polite 'Sie gestatten, mein Herr?' seated myself opposite.

He grunted permission, watching me with puzzled eyes. He did not seem over-burdened with intelligence, but I was not going to fall into the error of under-rating my opponent.

'Pray forgive me,' I began, 'but I have an idea that you are interested in me. May I ask why?'

This direct attack disconcerted him. He was momentarily at a loss, and continued to stare hard at me without speaking.

Then he said gruffly, 'Your papers, please.'

I had been hoping for this, and at the same time fearing it. I handed them over in silence.

He glanced through them, then put one or two questions that showed he had missed the one or two vital details that, to a mind more acute, would have suggested a doubt as to the genuineness of the papers. My relief was great, though the ordeal was not yet over.

'They seem to be in order,' he remarked, still retaining the papers. 'But the hotel clerk thought you were a foreigner.'

'That's not surprising. I have lived abroad for a great many years, and am now on a holiday before settling down again in the fatherland.'

At this juncture my companion condescended to accept a drink – a good sign. He was gradually thawing, but, as I could see, was not yet entirely satisfied. I discovered that he belonged to the Hamburg police. He frankly admitted that he was at Wangerooge to keep a look-out for spies.

'Have you caught any yet?' I inquired blandly.

'We keep our eyes open,' he answered evasively. 'It doesn't do for visitors to be too inquisitive in a fortified place like this. We don't want any Englishman spying round.'

'Well,' I said, 'you haven't answered my first question. Why were you particularly interested in me?'

'I had reason to be when the hotel man said he thought you were a foreigner, although using a German name. Foreigners are not welcome here, and if they choose to come they cannot complain if we see they don't get into mischief. All this coast is infested with English spies.'

We talked for half an hour quite amicably, but at the end of that time I was still not sure that his suspicions were allayed. I could do nothing more, and finally left him, saying that I wanted a walk before catching the steamer back to Harle. This sailed at 6.30 p.m., but I knew that the NDL boat from Norderney to Bremen called at Wangerooge about 4.30 p.m., and had privately determined to leave by that – always assuming I was permitted to do so.

Calling at the hotel to collect my rucksack, I mentioned that I proposed to catch the Harle steamer. Then I set out for the beach again, and, once clear of the village, increased my pace, keeping parallel with the shore.

Having gone about a mile, I stopped and glanced back. There were several people near, but my friend the detective was not among them.

The pier was now only a mile away, and the Bremen boat was not due for another hour. So I remained where I was until the last fifteen minutes, still seeing no sign of my 'shadow', and then walked briskly towards the pier. Five minutes after I got there the steamer came in, and I went on board with a crowd of passengers. The boat did not cast off at once, and the ten minutes she remained alongside were rather trying. But the detective did not make his appearance, nobody took the slightest notice of me, and eventually we were off.

At Bremerhaven, which we reached after dark, I had another mild scare, for there were two policemen on the dock when the gangway was lowered. But apparently they were not there for any special purpose, and did not attempt to come on board. We arrived at Bremen towards 11 p.m., and I just caught the last train to Hamburg, feeling safer in that great city, with its large transient population.

I have no doubt that the Wangerooge detective went to the pier to see me off by the Harle boat, and that when I did not show up all his former suspicions were re-awakened. But whatever steps he may subsequently have taken were ineffectual, for I was not interfered with in any way. Nevertheless, he had interrupted my programme and forced me to withdraw from the coast.

Three months later I was back again, and this time made a thorough job of it, visiting Wilhelmshaven – the main German naval base, with a dockyard four times as large as that at Kiel; Heligoland, where I obtained a close-up view of the four double 12-inch-gun turrets and the mortar battery on the Oberland, besides inspecting the new harbour works and naval establishments; Cuxhaven, with its naval station at Groden, the sea forts of Neuwerk, Kugelbake, and Grimmerhorn, and the batteries at Neues Fort and Döse – most of which were within plain view; Brunsbuettel, at the North Sea entrance of the Kiel Canal, to see the gigantic new locks then in course of construction, the new 6-inch gun battery, and the near-by fort of Neufeld; Geestemünde, a big submarine mining depôt at the mouth of the Weser; and, finally, the island of Sylt.

I am revealing no secret when I say that our war plans visualised an attack on Sylt, either as a feint in the hope of enticing out the German fleet, or as a serious assault intended to give us possession of the island for use as a base for military raids into Schleswig-Holstein.

I spent a week at Sylt, and was able to make a detailed report *not only on the defences then existing, but also on those that were projected. Indeed, reports compiled from the data on the German North Sea coastal defences, which I collected that summer and autumn, made up a respectable volume that, if it were published, would even today cause a sensation in Germany and lead to violent heart-searchings on the part of many German officials – assuming them still to survive – under whose very noses this mass of information had been gathered.*

CHAPTER 11

FAMOUS 'SPY' TRIALS

NEXT TO THE Dreyfus affair, the outstanding cause célèbre connected with espionage in modern times was undoubtedly the Brandon–Trench case of May 1910. Many other incidents of the same kind occurred in Germany during the four years just preceding the war, but none caught the public interest to an equal extent.

At that time a violent epidemic of spy mania was raging in Germany, and it is probably safe to say that not one in a dozen of the suspects who were arrested had any association with British intelligence work at all. Yet these unfortunate people served England well, if inadvertently, because while the German security department was occupied in tracking these quite unimportant visitors it was overlooking the men who really mattered to us.

At their trial before the Supreme Court at Leipzig in December 1910, Captain Bernard Trench, RMLI, and Lieutenant Vivian Brandon, RN, admitted freely that they visited Germany with the intention of collecting information on military matters and communicating the results of their investigations to the naval intelligence department at the admiralty.

That is a point that is often forgotten in connection with the trial, and a legend has grown up that the two officers were innocent victims of spy mania.

Their own story, as told at the trial, quite disposes of that idea.

Captain Trench, speaking German quite easily, said that he had been seconded for a period in Copenhagen to study Danish. He had then been joined by Lieutenant Brandon, and between them they had planned a tour in Germany, visiting Kiel, Cuxhaven, Bremen, Heligoland, Norderney and other islands of the same group, and finishing up at Borkum.

The arrangement was that they should meet at Brunsbuettel, at the North Sea end of the Kiel Canal. At that place Captain Trench received from his companion a list of questions, which he answered, with regard to certain small quick-firing guns. On his way to Bremen *via* Bremerhaven he inspected the position of the fortifications at the mouth of the River Weser and then proceeded to the island of Sylt. Subsequently he spent two or three days in Norderney and thence visited Wangerooge.

'What was interesting there?' asked the presiding judge.

'There is a church tower at the end of the island, which seems curious, as that part of the island is uninhabited,' Captain Trench answered.

He and Brandon visited Borkum together, and on the way to inspect the searchlight station they became separated. Captain Trench entered one of the batteries without hindrance. When he came out he met Lieutenant Brandon, whom he told to go in and have a look. This the lieutenant did, and was arrested.

Captain Trench was not detained at that time. The two officers were allowed by the police to meet. They talked, it appeared, about the battery and how the information they had gained was to be passed on to 'Reggie'. Furthermore, incriminating papers were seized in Trench's room at a hotel in Emden, whereupon he, too, was arrested.

Several mysterious figures were referred to in the course of the evidence, of whom 'Reggie' was one.

Lieutenant Brandon said that this was not his friend's real name, but Captain Trench admitted that 'Reggie' was connected with the intelligence department of the British Admiralty. (It may be mentioned as a curious coincidence that the director of naval intelligence during the war was Admiral Sir Reginald Hall, but his nickname in the navy was not 'Reggie', but 'Blinker'.)

Although neither of the accused would disclose the actual identity of 'Reggie', they were very frank about him in other ways, admitting that his private telegraphic address was 'Sunburnt, London', and that they had asked him to meet them at Delfzyl, just across the border in Holland, at the end of their visit to Borkum.

Another mystery figure was 'Charles', whom Lieutenant Brandon claimed was himself, while a 'John Birch' mentioned in their correspondence was claimed by Captain Trench as his own alias.

One of the disclosures that caused most sensation in Germany was a statement by the accused that the British Admiralty possessed a 'Naval Baedeker'. This book was stated to be a private compilation, available only to naval officers, containing information about the German coast and coastal defences.

Some idea of the class of information contained in it was disclosed in the course of the evidence.

Thus, Lieutenant Brandon was, admittedly, a surveying officer in the British Navy, and he had with him at the time of the visit to Germany photographic and surveying instruments. Captain Taegert, IGN, the expert called for the German government, said that the notes found in the possession of the accused contained information about the length and width of landing stages and depth of water at Sylt, Amrum, and other islands. Notes made by Captain Trench were read out in court, but with certain figures and names omitted. One memorandum read as follows:

> *Breakwaters, coal sheds, coal stores here. There are no cranes. Railway lines by bridge. Bridge x yards long x yards wide. Cement wall all round promenade. Wells in all villages. Indifferent roads. White reefs not visible at flood tide.*

In regard to Wangerooge there was a note in Lieutenant Brandon's writing:

> *Landing piers x high, x long, x broad. Milk and eggs come from the mainland. Only five buildings on the west side. Seen no building that can contain mines. The beacon furthest out is occupied and has telegraphs.*

An interesting point developed in regard to Wangerooge. The German expert declared that the notes on the fortifications there were a most serious matter, as they were treated with the utmost secrecy officially. Lieutenant Brandon countered this by claiming that his attention was drawn to the subject by an article in a German paper, which he had read in London.

Captain Taegert also pointed out that at Cuxhaven the accused had taken angles from a dyke, with two churches on the mainland and the position of the fortifications entered on the map in accordance with these observations. Captain Taegert added that he had examined the measurements and found them extraordinarily accurate.

On the sketches dealing with Heligoland, he continued, the quick-firing battery was marked, with measurements of the distances between some of the gun positions. The distances from the extremities of the batteries to the lighthouse were also measured. Further, the gun positions on the south-east and north-west were accurately sketched.

The contention of the defence was that the soundings taken around Sylt and other Frisian Islands were intended for public admiralty charts, issued for the use of pinnaces and other small craft belonging to British warships that visited German North Sea ports in time of peace.

Captain Trench said that his report on Cuxhaven was actually compiled in England from the 'Naval Baedeker', and Lieutenant Brandon stated that he had a list of questions to answer with regard to that place. It was not compulsory to answer any of the questions derived from the 'Naval Baedeker'. Officers who travelled could answer them or not as they chose.

To this defence the prosecution replied, through Captain Taegert, that English warships had never entered those waters in time of peace, and consequently there could be no object in compiling notes for the purpose alleged. In landing operations, he declared, Sylt would become of prime importance as a *point d'appui*, and the landing stage on the island had been measured and photographed in great detail by the accused. They had, moreover, noted the shallows while bathing.

Counsel for the defence suggested that the measurements of depths made in this way could be of no importance, as the tides were not taken into account. Captain Taegert could not agree, pointing out that the measurements were not merely estimated, but were actually taken.

From the final speeches for the prosecution it became clear that the idea that all this information was collected with a view to facilitating a sudden British naval attack on the German North Sea coast had been impressed on the court during one of the sittings held in camera. For political reasons, most of the proceedings took place in public; indeed, the imperial prosecutor had asked at the first session that this should be so. But on the morning of the second and last day of the trial there was a lengthy secret sitting, at which military and general staff experts gave evidence.

It was noteworthy that the prosecution throughout treated the accused with marked mildness, and did not press for the full rigour of the law. Indeed, in his final address to the court, Dr Zweigert, the imperial prosecutor, said that the fact of the prisoners being foreigners who had acted in the interests of their own country, under the direct orders of the intelligence service, might be regarded as extenuating circumstances. The accused had denied the imputed connections, but counsel thought they had done so from honourable motives.

The circumstance that they had never sought to induce Germans to assist them, and had made a partial confession, also mitigated the gravity of the charge. He therefore asked that Captain Trench and Lieutenant Brandon should each be sentenced, not to penal servitude, but to imprisonment in a fortress for six years, two and a half months of the time during which they had been in custody to be included.

The fifteen judges – all robed in long purple gowns with velvet facings, and wearing quaint round purple velvet caps – retired, the president, Judge Menge, leading the way. He was a man of patriarchal appearance, with a flowing snow-white beard.

They were absent for two hours considering their judgment. Dusk was falling in the crowded courthouse as they filed in again. A single chandelier suspended from the high ceiling was the only source of light in the court room as Judge Menge announced judgment and sentence.

The verdict was guilty, and the sentence four years' detention in a fortress.

It is important to note the difference between penal servitude (a criminal sentence) and fortress detention (an officers' punishment that involves no professional dishonour). The German law provides that either form of sentence may be inflicted in cases of espionage. That the Leipzig Court chose the milder way, as suggested by the imperial prosecutor, showed that diplomatic considerations had prevailed in the case.

There was a certain significance, too, in the comments of the German papers at the time. On the day after the trial, for example, the *Berliner Tageblatt* said:

> *The two Englishmen only committed an offence that is regularly committed by numerous officers of all countries, and apart from this their bearing in court left an extremely favourable impression on every one. Having had the misfortune to be caught, they took no trouble to deny what was evident; while at the same time they frankly refused to say anything that would compromise a third person or cause any embarrassment to their own naval authorities. Their attitude deserves all respect. We hope the two gentlemen*

will not be obliged to remain in a German fortress too long ...
and that at some suitable opportunity –certainly not later than
King George's coronation – the remainder of their sentence will
be remitted.

This prophecy, if it were not inspired, was certainly a signal instance of intelligent anticipation on the part of the editor. The actual pardon by the Kaiser was delayed until May 1913, and was then granted on the occasion of the visit of King George to Berlin to attend the wedding of the Kaiser's only daughter.

They had then served two years and five months of the sentence, Captain Trench at Glatz and Lieutenant Brandon first at Wesel and subsequently at Königsberg.

Both officers were actively engaged during the war. For part of the time Major Trench was base intelligence officer at Queenstown, busily occupied in the work of tracking German submarines at sea.

Captain Brandon, as he came to be, was assistant director of naval intelligence at the admiralty in 1918.

There was a world of difference between the Brandon–Trench affair and the next famous 'espionage' case in Germany – the Bertrand Stewart episode. In the first-named case the German authorities may be said to have stumbled quite accidentally across the accused. In the second, the alleged spy was the victim of a deliberate plot to entangle him. He was betrayed to the Germans by an *agent provocateur* specially detailed for the work, and, as is made evident by the published judgment of the court that tried him, no actual case was ever proved against him. Mr Bertrand Stewart himself always protested his innocence. Nevertheless, he was condemned and sentenced, remaining in confinement for rather more than a year before he, too, was pardoned by the Kaiser at the same time as Brandon and Trench.

The Stewart case is a striking example of the perils that surrounded the intelligence agent who was working in Germany. It exposed to public gaze the network of counter-espionage that the German authorities had built up, and it showed how vitally necessary it was for the intelligence man to work almost wholly on his own. If he made any use of outside assistance, if he took information from other people at all, he had to be absolutely satisfied of their good faith before entering into any sort of negotiations with them.

The story of the Stewart case was summarised so clearly in the court's judgment that it cannot be better told than in these words:

> *The first thing that concerns us is that he procured the exact address in a small place of a man whom he used as agent for his espionage purposes. He promised this man £100 if the latter declared himself ready to act as agent in the transmission of news, and prisoner eventually adopted a false address where his correspondence could be delivered.*
>
> *On the evening of 29 July 1911, the accused travelled from London and sought out this agent in Germany. He had a long conversation with him, in the course of which the prisoner handed over to the agent a first payment – namely, £5. On a later occasion he gave him a further sum of £10…*
>
> *After the agent had again returned to Bremen, on 31 July, about five o'clock in the morning, the prisoner held a long conversation with him in the waiting room, and the agent made him an exhaustive report. Next day the prisoner left Hamburg and visited*

Cuxhaven, was also in Heligoland, and then returned via Wil-
helmshaven and Bremerhaven to Bremen.

At Bremen, on the night of 1 August, he had another long con-
versation with the agent in a waiting room of the railway station.
The agent, who likewise had been making inquiries in the mean-
time, submitted to the prisoner on this occasion a drawing that
provided information relating to the preparedness of the Ger-
man fleet in the North Sea. The prisoner took this report, read it
through, and then tore it up and threw it aside.

Shortly after this the prisoner was arrested in Bremen.

Nothing more has been proved against the prisoner in the course
of the trial. There has been, in particular, no confirmation in the
trial of the rumours that suggested that the prisoner, acting under
the orders of the English Information service, had collected impor-
tant secrets in Germany by bribery. The prisoner's journey and
his transactions were rather the result, as he himself has submit-
ted, of his own initiative…

As far as the verdict is concerned, it may be left an open question
whether the prisoner or his agent would in reality have succeeded
in determining the disposition of the ships in the North Sea in the
summer of 1911. It may also be left an open question what really
were the contents of the agent's report that the prisoner tore up.

Stewart was found guilty of an attempt to unearth military secrets,
but his patriotic motive was a circumstance that weighed in his
favour, and he was sentenced to detention in a fortress for three
years and six months, reduced by four months on account of
the period of his detention while awaiting trial.

The sentence roused intense indignation in Great Britain.
Undoubtedly the judgment rested upon an extremely weak case,

leaving a great number of pertinent questions unanswered. This trial, unlike that of Brandon and Trench, was held in camera throughout, only the judgment being made public; but later on enough information was forthcoming from various sources to make it clear that the whole case for the prosecution rested on the evidence of the *agent provocateur*.

Who was this man?

He was a Belgian, calling himself Frederic Rue, but his real name was Arsène Marie Verrue. He was born at Courtrai on 14 February 1861.

British investigators soon got on the track of his record, when it was discovered that he had been sentenced on several occasions for robbery and for assault with violence. He had at one time run a soap factory, but had gone bankrupt, the official records of the bankruptcy in 1894 being marked by the Tribunal 'non-excusable'. Later he was representative in Belgium for a British brewery company, which in 1905 charged him with appropriating cheques given to him for the payment of creditors and with forging the endorsements thereto.

He disappeared, but was tried in his absence and sentenced to four terms of six months each on the various counts.

Publication of these facts did nothing to allay feeling in Britain. Evidence from such a tainted source was felt to be inadmissible. Further investigation soon established that Verrue was certainly in the pay of the Brussels spy bureau, of which we already had some knowledge, and of which a man calling himself R. H. Peterssen was the head. He had other names – Müller, Pieters, Schmidt, and Talbot among them.

While this bureau was partly an international exchange for the naval and military secrets of every country, it was also made use of by the German authorities for purposes of counter-espionage. There was a definite scale of charges, among them one of £4 5s. for the betrayal of an intelligence man working in Germany. It was never definitely established that the plot that led to the arrest of Stewart was fomented by the German authorities, but there was no doubt that the trap had been deliberately laid by Peterssen.

The British intelligence department knew a great deal about Herr Peterssen. He had planted spies in Britain for Germany. Only a short time before the Stewart case his name had been mentioned in public court, in the course of the trial at Winchester Assizes of Heinrich Grosse, who was there found guilty of espionage.

The information we had was that Peterssen was in receipt of a regular monthly salary from German sources of £50 and expenses, and was paid a bonus of £4 5s for every spy detected in Germany through his organisation.

Peterssen was not particularly successful. His methods were so crude and blatant that much came to be known about his activities. He advertised freely in the Belgian papers, offering to buy information. He could do this with impunity, because there was at that time no law against espionage in Belgium.

One of his advertisements was answered by a sergeant in the Belgian army who found himself in monetary difficulties. Peterssen asked him for information about certain Belgian fortresses. This the sergeant could not provide, but he offered to furnish documents relating to French mobilisation.

Herr Peterssen rubbed his hands. This was a splendid catch. He arranged for the sergeant to get the documents and proceed to a small suburban station outside Brussels, there to meet a man who would come from Aix-la-Chapelle.

Now, Aix is very near the frontier, and after leaving Peterssen's office, the sergeant began to dislike the whole business. While the cold fit was still on him he went to M Victor Darsac, then editor of the great Brussels evening paper *Le Soir*, and told him the whole story.

M Darsac acted promptly. He at once informed the authorities, and in agreement with them arranged to send a crowd of reporters and photographers to the suburban railway station at the appointed time, to be present at the interview.

The German agent duly arrived to meet the sergeant.

He met him – but he also met the local municipal authorities, who gave him a mock civic welcome, while the camera men photographed the scene and the reporters made copious notes.

And in the courtyard in front of the station a Belgian military band ironically played '*Die Wacht Am Rhein*' for his edification.

It was a glorious comedy – with no tragic results for anybody, since there was no law against espionage. But the German agent went back to Aix-la-Chapelle and beyond in a very bad temper, doubtless feeling as much of a fool as any German secret service agent could be made to feel.

The outcry in Britain against the condemnation of Stewart evoked, of course, an equally bitter response in Germany.

In an interview published by the *Hamburger Nachrichten*, Verrue denied point blank all the allegations made against him.

His own story was that he was paid by both the British and German governments, but that he found the British so niggardly and the Germans so generous that 'he conceived it to be his duty to save Germany from the effects of British espionage'.

Exactly what fees Verrue received has never been established. Mr Stewart after his release expressed the opinion that, from beginning to end, the German government paid £1,000 for the evidence that procured his sentence.

The Bertrand Stewart case is perhaps the most dramatic instance of the *agent provocateur*'s part in secret service work that has ever become known outside the innermost circles. Of Stewart's innocence, legally, there was never any question. At the most, he ventured indiscreetly into places from which any foreign visitor to Germany in the year 1911 would have been well advised to keep away unless he had business there.

Stewart's own story was that at Cuxhaven he walked along the public road adjoining the harbour for twenty minutes, after asking two German officers if this was permitted and being answered in the affirmative. In Heligoland he walked for eighteen minutes in the public street without speaking to anyone. In Wilhelmshaven he walked alone, quickly and without stopping, from the steamboat pier to the railway station through the public streets.

British indignation, however, had very little effect beyond adding to the bitterness of feeling between the two countries, and even the pardon by the Kaiser – graciously timed as it was to coincide with the visit of the King and Queen to Berlin – did not remove the unpleasant impression produced by the whole circumstances of the case.

Stewart, who was a keen Yeomanry officer, was promoted to a captaincy in the West Kent Yeomanry a few weeks after he returned to England. When war broke out he was appointed to the headquarters staff of Major-General Allenby, and went straight to France with the Expeditionary Force. This fulfilled the prophecy (it was more than a wish) he uttered at the close of his trial in Leipzig: 'If your distinguished country ever attacks mine I hope to be among those who take part in the fight. Even if my own regiment is not called out I should endeavour to serve with another cavalry regiment.'

He was serving in the intelligence branch of the Cavalry Division when, in September 1914, he was shot dead while reconnoitring up in the firing line.

There were scores of other spy cases in Germany in the three years that preceded the war, but none possessed the dramatic interest of the two we have recorded above. Many of them were pettifogging affairs, several being due solely to indiscretion on the part of adventurous spirits. One case, which might well have led to an international incident of first-class importance, never came to a head.

It arose out of an almost incredibly unwise rowing-boat excursion by the late Lord Brassey in Kiel Harbour.

During Kiel Week, 1914, when the British Second Battle Squadron, under Sir George Warrender, with its attendant cruisers and small craft, was officially visiting Kiel, Lord Brassey was present in his yacht *Sunbeam*. The story was told, and, from the German point of view, very well told, by one of the liaison officers with the British staff, Commander von Hase:

> *While rowing in one of the small boats from his yacht, Lord Brassey entered the submarine harbour of the imperial dockyard, where no civilians are admitted and where several of our latest submarines were lying. Here he was arrested by a dockyard policeman and detained for several hours in the guardroom. Not until he was able to establish his identity through a German officer known to him was he released by order of the dockyard representative. There was widespread indignation in Kiel at Lord*

*Brassey's gross tactlessness, and the Kaiser also expressed him-
self pretty sharply on the subject.*

To appreciate fully the 'tactlessness' to which Commander
von Hase refers, it must be borne in mind that Lord Brassey
was the founder and editor of what was then perhaps the most
famous naval annual in the world. He was known as one of the
keenest civilian students of international developments, and he
was a foremost advocate of British naval strength.

In view of these circumstances, there was little likelihood
that he would try to act as a secret service agent, but the incident is worth recalling as an example of the kind of blunder
that helped to keep spy fever alive in Germany.

Glancing through the records of all the espionage trials that
took place in Germany between 1911 and 1914, one very interesting fact reveals itself to those who know what was happening
behind the scenes.

The Germans, as mentioned elsewhere in these pages, never
caught any of the men who were regularly doing naval intelligence work for Britain.

This may fairly be claimed as a testimony to the skill of those
men. The whole country was on the alert to detect 'spies'. An
extensive and well-organised counter-espionage bureau was
continually on the watch. Snare after snare was laid for people
who roused the slightest suspicion about their activities. The
naval ports bristled with booby traps for their benefit.

They escaped them all, and they got away with the news.

Their names will never be known. Today the few survivors
of that service find their only excitement in a debate in committee at the golf club, or in the purchase of a sweepstake ticket

under the eyes of a local JP. That is about the wildest extrava-gance they can afford on their 'savings'.

Secret service work does not pay – whether you are caught or not.

CHAPTER 12

WATCHING THE
HIGH SEAS FLEET

HIDDEN AWAY IN the depths of the massive *Blue Book* (published in 1920) containing the despatches, reports, and signals relating to the Battle of Jutland, is an audacious disclosure of something that might well be regarded as an official secret of the first importance.

As an introduction to the long record of signals and orders issued during the sixty hours or so that the Jutland operations lasted, from the time the Grand Fleet put to sea to its return to Scapa Flow, the following note appears in the Blue Book:

> *On 30 May 1916, the admiralty received news that pointed to early activity on the part of the German fleet. Admiralty telegram No. 434 of 30 May 1916, time of origin 1740, sent to the Commander-in-Chief and repeated to the Vice-Admiral commanding battlecruiser*

fleet, contained the following instructions: 'You should proceed to 1 Eastward of Long Forties ready for eventualities.'

It is important to remember the time of origin of that message to Admiral Jellicoe. It was 5.40 p.m. on 30 May. The German High Seas Fleet did not begin to weigh anchor until 3 a.m. the next day, ten hours later. It follows, therefore, that twelve hours before a move was made by the enemy our intelligence department knew that it was going to be made. And after the war the admiralty had no scruple about making public the fact that they did know.

This was but one of several occasions on which we had advance information of the enemy's movements.

The Battle of the Dogger Bank on 24 January 1915, was no mere chance encounter. On the day before the action the battle-cruisers were lying at anchor in the Firth of Forth, having only just returned from a sweep down towards the Bight of Heligoland. They had been in harbour rather less than forty-eight hours when the ID got news that Hipper's battlecruisers were coming out for a raid on the East Coast. Although that information was not received twelve hours before the enemy started, the Battle-cruiser fleet reached the spot in plenty of time.

It was due to a combination of several factors that our naval intelligence service was able to maintain a constant watch on the High Seas Fleet. A very useful element in the system was directional wireless, coupled with our possession of the German codebooks found in the wreck of the cruiser *Magdeburg*.

Directional wireless enabled us to locate pretty accurately the position of the German Commander-in-Chief from day to day, and from hour to hour, as he communicated with his various

squadrons and flotillas by wireless, while the code books enabled us to interpret what he was saying – as long, that is, as the
Germans continued to employ the same code, which, to our
astonishment, they did for over a year. It had been changed
before Jutland, however.

Directional wireless, of course, had its risks, as we found
during the Battle of Jutland, when calculations based on this
system placed Scheer still in Wilhelmshaven roadstead with
his fleet when actually he was well out at sea in support of
Hipper's battlecruisers. The German Commander-in-Chief
tricked us neatly that time. Probably he suspected the use we
were making of directional wireless. Certainly, by that time the
Germans themselves had made some progress in its use, though
their methods were still elementary. Scheer took the precaution of transferring his flagship's wavelength and code call to
a depot ship that was still lying at Wilhelmshaven. And as we
still got that call in the same strength from the same direction,
we naturally assumed Scheer to be still in harbour.

Although he caught us napping on this occasion, no particular harm was done, as it happened, because our own battle
fleet was at sea in support of Beatty's Battlecruiser Force, and
there was consequently no fear of him being overwhelmed by
the entire naval strength of Germany.

Then again, our submarines in the Bight were very efficient
news-gatherers. From midnight on 4 August 1914, till midday
on 11 November 1918, the exits from Wilhelmshaven, Cuxhaven, and Emden were never for an hour without a British
undersea sentinel. The intelligence department was largely
concerned in the organisation of this patrol, for the real object
of the boats in the Bight came to be, at the request of the

department, the gathering of news even more than the taking of offensive action.

As our submarines in the early days were equipped only with short-range wireless, any information they sent had to be relayed. It is perhaps hardly realised by the younger generation how rapidly wireless has developed since 1914. In that year the record range for transmission from a submarine was set up by the German boat *U-27*, which got a message through to her depot ship from a distance of 140 miles. And that happened under particularly favourable circumstances.

By 1916, however, our submarines were equipped with high-power wireless, and thereafter their captains were strictly enjoined, when on patrol in the Bight, not to attack the German High Seas Fleet *on its way out of harbour*. They were to note the composition of the squadrons, their course, and other relative matters, and, when the ships had passed, rise to the surface and report by wireless at once.

Then, if the enemy heard the wireless, guessed what was happening, and turned back, the submarines were free to do all the attacking they liked; but outward-bound ships had to be left alone, in the hope that they would fall into the hands of the Grand Fleet.

The scheme worked very well as a whole, but sometimes the results were disappointing, as the following example will show. The German battle fleet put to sea on 23 April 1918, and steered northward towards Horn Reefs, just outside its mined waters. Submarine *U-6* was on patrol in the vicinity. She observed the enemy ships approaching, but, mistaking them for British, allowed them to pass unmolested and sent in no report of any kind to the Commander-in-Chief. On the following day, however, the same submarine saw the High Seas Fleet returning, and this time identified it correctly. After watching its passage for several hours she flashed a message to Admiral Beatty.

Meanwhile another submarine, *E-42*, had also sighted the German ships, and as they were obviously returning to port, she was at liberty to attack them. Four torpedoes were fired, one of which struck the *Moltke*. The damage was so serious that only after a precarious towing operation was the great battlecruiser able to reach port.

Besides maintaining their watch on the High Seas Fleet, the British submarines in the Bight were also useful in keeping us informed about the German minefields.

When German minelayers came out to lay a new field in some hitherto safe area of water, they were almost always seen, the whole of their operations followed, and the exact bearings and limits of the new field reported to the admiralty within an hour or two. Then another little red patch would be marked on the confidential charts, and all ships at sea were warned to avoid the new danger spot.

When the Allies took over control of the German ports after the Armistice, the German Admiral Meurer, who negotiated the terms of surrender with Admiral Beatty on board the *Queen Elizabeth*, was required to produce charts of all the German minefields for our safe guidance. On comparing these charts with our own we found that we knew the exact position and extent of every German minefield then in existence. The Germans, on their part, were by no means so well informed.

When Admiral Meurer was ordered to the Firth of Forth to open negotiations, we gave him a course to steer and fixed a rendezvous at which he was to meet our escorting cruiser. He was late at the rendezvous, and explained that he had had to make a wide detour to avoid a German minefield that lay right across the course we had given him. The Grand Fleet staff officers chuckled. That particular minefield had been swept up long before – and the Germans did not know it had gone.

In another case, comedy blended with tragedy. A German minefield had been laid in the Straits of Dover. We had detected it, and were about to sweep it up when it became known that two U-boats were in the Straits. We immediately decided to carry out a 'dummy' sweep – that is, to go over the area as though we were sweeping, but actually to leave the mines where they were. The trick worked. One of the German U-boats, thinking to find a safe route through the perils of the Dover defile, closely followed the minesweepers – and blew up on a German mine! By chance the captain was rescued from the wreck, and was Teutonically indignant at the trick that had been played on him!

Nor was it only at sea that a watch was kept on the German High Seas Fleet. There were British agents in the German naval bases from whom we received priceless information. The men who did that work deserved well of their country, and it would be interesting to know whether any one of them ever received a decoration.

Needless to say, such work was far more hazardous in war than in peacetime. Moreover, it called for an even higher standard of reliability.

In war false news can easily lead to disaster, yet there is neither the time nor the opportunity to verify it, as may be possible in peace. There were one or two false alarms during the war that caused grave anxiety at ID headquarters.

One bad winter's night our forces were sent dashing out

into the North Sea on a definite course in chase of a reported enemy squadron, whose prospective movements for twelve hours had just been communicated to us. In point of fact, as we discovered much later, that particular squadron actually was at sea and followed the course indicated; but owing to fog our ships missed it by about 3 miles, and the enemy returned to harbour without us knowing for certain that he had really been at sea at all.

The days following that abortive chase were trying ones for the ID.

Had the whole business been a trap for certain of our agents in Germany?

Had the news been allowed to leak out in certain directions for the purpose of enabling the German authorities to trace the sources of leakage and stop them for ever?

It was a deadly, wearing week. We decided not to communicate with our men at all, even by the safest routes, lest they should be already under suspicion. If they were, anything we did might provide just the last scrap of evidence their watchers needed. We had to wait patiently for them to communicate with us again – if they could. Those at the head of the secret service went through keen mental torture during that week. It was not only the painful feeling that tried and devoted helpers might have paid the supreme penalty for their loyalty. There was the complex problem of replacing them, if the worst had happened.

The tension was broken on a Sunday morning, when further news came through from the source from which we had been warned of the cruise.

No reference was made to any trouble or any undue suspicion directed towards that source. The ID chiefs breathed again.

These agents ashore did not always have to work at lightning speed. One of the noteworthy things about the German command at sea, which we came to recognise as time went on, was the length of the preparations they made for any sortie.

For example, nine days before the Battle of the Dogger Bank we received definite information that 'liveliness' was to be expected. For some reason, both Kiel, which is on the Baltic, and Wilhelmshaven, in the Bight, were in a state of unusual activity. One report told us that two battlecruisers had left the Jade, but then followed a period of quiescence, and it began to look as though the alarm had been a false one. But on the morning of 23 January the thermometer went up again. More news, and urgent news, came through. The Bight was boiling up.

Mr Winston Churchill, who, as First Lord of the Admiralty, had unique opportunities of watching naval intelligence work from behind the scenes, tells the story in *The World Crisis*:

> *It was nearly noon when I regained my room in the admiralty. I had hardly sat down when the door opened quickly and in marched Sir Arthur Wilson, unannounced. He looked at me intently, and there was a glow in his eye. Behind him came Oliver with charts and compasses.*
>
> *'First Lord, those fellows are coming out again.'*
> *'When?'*
> *'Tonight. We have just time to get Beatty there.'*

Mr Churchill then records the various telegrams of instruction sent to Commodore Tyrwhitt, Admirals Beatty and Jellicoe, and continues: 'This done, Sir Arthur explained briefly the conclusions he had formed from the intercepted German message, which our cryptographers had translated, and from other intelligence of which he was a master.'

The deduction made from the various items of information by the ID and the Operations Division was that another coastal raid was in preparation, though all that our reports told us was that a scouting expedition towards the Dogger Bank was in view. Accordingly, the Commander-in-Chief and the Vice-Admiral Commanding the Battlecruisers were both informed that four German battlecruisers, six light cruisers, and twenty-two destroyers were to sail that night to scout on the Dogger Bank, probably returning on the following evening. The British forces were therefore ordered to rendezvous in 55.13 N. 3.12 E. at 7 a.m. on the 24th.

It may seem something like wizardry to those not versed in intelligence work that our agents should have been able to advise us so exactly of the composition of the German forces. Perhaps, in order to heighten the colour, it ought to be pretended that a British agent was working as confidential secretary on the staff of the German Commander-in-Chief!

It was, however, not necessary to go to such lengths to discover what was in the wind. Activity in the dockyard and the basins in connection with certain ships, orders or counter-orders to certain purveyors of stores, the postponement of a *Bier-Abend* by the officers of a half-flotilla, the marshalling of drafts at the naval barracks – these were the straws that showed the skilled intelligence man the line of investigation to pursue.

He knew some facts from which he could safely draw certain conclusions. Incidents, which to the simple German shopkeeper or the gossip in the *Weinstube* meant nothing, were full of significance to the man trained in naval observation.

To take an example from our own experience: the night before the Dogger Bank battle it was known all over Edinburgh that the battlecruisers were going out, partly because of the sudden departure early in the afternoon of officers who were on shore and the procession of taxicabs taking them to Hawes Pier, partly because of the countermanding of orders for provisions from various messmen. The difference was that in our case no German agent seems to have got the news, or, if he did, was unable to transmit it to Germany in time to be of service to his side.

The position was much the same on the eve of the Battle of Jutland.

Admiral Scheer began to plan the 'enterprise towards the north', which led to that battle at least three weeks beforehand. His own report (accessible to us long afterwards, of course) indicates that he had two plans in view: one, a bombardment of Sunderland; the other, a demonstration off the Skagerrak. He actually made the initial move in his operations a fortnight before the battle took place, when he sent out U-boats to lie off the Firth of Forth, Cromarty, and Scapa Flow. Part of their mission was to ambush the Grand Fleet, but they were also to enact the rôle of scouts, just as our submarines operated in the Bight.

These movements of German submarines became known to us, and it was not long before we had each group located. The fact that they were lurking in areas not prolific in mercantile targets was significant, and fully confirmed the suggestions of our agents in the German ports.

An essential element of Scheer's Sunderland scheme was airship reconnaissance; but weather conditions from 15 May onwards made that impossible, and from day to day he delayed sailing. In the end he was compelled to make a move by the fact that his submarines were approaching the limit of their cruising orders. As weather conditions still kept the Zeppelin scouts in their sheds, he had to follow the alternative of an advance to the north, a mere demonstration. And as we studied the weather conditions as closely as he did, it was not difficult, once we knew he was on the move, to judge the direction in which he was steering.

Apropos of weather conditions, the Germans had rather a neat piece of intelligence work to their credit. About noon on 31 May the Neumünster wireless station informed Scheer that a wireless signal from Scapa had been intercepted, giving a weather report for the North Sea. The Neumünster people added that they had noticed that such reports were only sent out when Jellicoe or Beatty were at sea in force. Although the information may not have been of much value to the German Commander-in-Chief, it is worth noting as typical of the infinitesimal detail that goes to the building up of a complete picture by intelligence experts. It also shows the unwisdom of cultivating too regular habits in wartime!

Scheer's other sources of information failed him badly. The reports from his submarine scouts were inadequate, containing little or no detail of ships seen, and it must have been impossible for his staff to have formed any definite idea of the whereabouts of Beatty and Jellicoe from such messages as they received.

So much for the German side.

On our side we had already, as it were, seen the red flag; but the High Seas Fleet had been so long inactive that it seemed too much to hope that the picture we had built up from our various reports and deductions was about to materialise.

However, the morning of 30 May brought pregnant news. At

10.48 a.m. (German time) a wireless signal was made by Scheer ordering all German vessels to concentrate in the outer roads of Wilhelmshaven at eight o'clock that night. That wireless signal we picked up. It was in code, of course, and it has been said, with more or less official sanction, that we were unable to decipher it. Perhaps it would be more fair to the brilliant men who undertook the brain-wearing task of reading cryptic ciphers for us to say that the version they produced could only be regarded as partial guesswork that was not accepted 'officially'.

At all events, when the German official history came out, with an appendix of the chief signals made by Scheer in the course of the action, those who, on that May morning in 1916, had concentrated all their mental efforts on the attempt to unravel the tangle of letters, discovered how nearly they had succeeded. The version given above is based on the official German wording, and not on the decoding.

The speed with which this particular department worked is perhaps indicated by the fact that at 11.58 GMT, or two hours and ten minutes after Scheer made the signal, the admiralty were already issuing warnings to those forces under their immediate jurisdiction (Dover Patrol, East Coast, and Thames Estuary), and it is fairly obvious that Jellicoe also was told something previous to the telegram of 5.40 p.m., because at the very moment that telegram is timed he hoisted the preparatory signal for putting to sea, as did the admiral in the Second Battle Squadron at Cromarty.

Reading between the lines of the official record of signals, there are good grounds for the inference that, whether or not the decoding was accepted officially, it was considered reliable enough to pass privately to the Commander-in-Chief for his information.

In his despatch on the Battle of Jutland published during the war, Admiral Jellicoe stated – no doubt for the purpose of misleading the enemy – that the Grand Fleet, 'in pursuance of the general policy of periodical sweeps through the North Sea, had left its bases on the previous day.' Consequently there has grown up in the public mind an idea that the meeting with the German High Seas Fleet, which we call the Battle of Jutland, was a purely accidental encounter – in other words, that we really 'muddled through' in our traditional fashion.

That assumption is grossly unfair to our intelligence men, and it is important to note that the misleading phrase quoted above is omitted from the final official version of the despatch, as published in 'Jutland Papers' in 1920. There full acknowledgment is made of the fact that the Grand Fleet proceeded to sea in consequence of information received.

There is much that still cannot be published as to the means by which that information was gathered, but it is due to the courageous agents who were stationed in enemy ports, and to the skilful men who used their brains to piece the fragments of news together, that public recognition should now be given to the fact that we knew Scheer was coming out and the direction he was likely to take.

CHAPTER 13

THE MEN WHO HEARD
THE U-BOATS TALK

S OME OF THE hardest work done by intelligence men
during the war had no spice of personal danger in it, but
for all that it was full of thrills.

Performed in the base intelligence offices at various points
round the coast, it was the cornerstone of the whole system by
which we countered the German submarine menace. The effectual use of the 5,000 patrol vessels and convoy craft, which were
engaged in the actual work of hunting the U-boats, depended
very largely on the intelligence men. It was the hard thinking
done in the base intelligence office that made possible the proper
planning of the dispositions of these anti-submarine craft.

It is, of course, a commonplace that the submarine's strongest
asset is the secrecy with which it can move from place to place.
The task of the base intelligence office was to get behind that

veil of secrecy; to determine, to within a mile or two, the where-abouts of every German submarine on any given day. And that knowledge referred, not only to the fifty or sixty boats actually at sea, either in northern waters, in the Channel, in the Atlantic or in the Mediterranean, but also to the others that had just gone back to port, those that were undergoing repairs, and those that were about to put to sea again.

At first sight this may seem an impossible task. How, it may be asked, could our intelligence people possibly know what was happening in the enemy dockyards of Wilhelmshaven and Kiel and Danzig during wartime? It was difficult enough to obtain any definite information about submarines during peacetime.

The task was not impossible, however. Indeed, by 1918 it had become almost as simple as a mathematical problem of the less abstruse order. In September of that year our intelligence people had a forecast of the dates on which every German sub-marine then in dockyard would reappear at sea. In every single instance the forecast was correct to within twenty-four hours.

Intelligence work of this kind is largely a matter of common sense, used by a mind trained to weigh the value and the mean-ing of the smallest clue. It depends upon accurate deduction. If one can imagine Sherlock Holmes solving a mystery without moving from his rooms in Baker Street, working solely by the accurate piecing together of little items of news given to him by this person or that, one has a rough idea of the way the base intelligence office grappled with the difficulty of keeping track of the U-boats.

The sources of information were many and varied. The most valuable of all were the wireless directional stations round our coasts. Directional wireless has, of course, made remarkable

strides since those days, but even then we had developed it sufficiently to gather accurate news day by day from the enemy's
own transmitting sets.

Reduced to its simplest terms, the method was this. A U-boat
somewhere off the north of Ireland called up a consort with
whom she had a rendezvous. One of our wireless directional
stations on the Scottish coast would hear her call. We will label
that Station X.

Another station on the north-east Irish coast would hear the
call. Label that Station Y.

And yet another station on the north-west Irish coast would
pick up the call. Label that Station Z.

Each of those stations would report to a central base intelligence office not only what it heard, but also the direction from
which the sounds were coming. The power of the sounds would
increase or decrease as a part of the receiving machine was turned
round by the operator. The point at which the signal strength
was most marked gave the bearing or direction of the source.

At the base intelligence office those reports would be worked
out on a large-scale chart. A line drawn from X, a line drawn
from Y, and a line drawn from Z in the direction that each station had reported, ought to meet somewhere.

Somewhere within a radius of about 2 miles or less round the
point where the three lines meet is the U-boat.

That was the simplest and easiest sort of problem for the intelligence officer. With only one U-boat calling there was not much
chance of confusion. When several calls were reported at the
same time, however, the problem became more difficult. Three
or four calls might be notified at about the same time, some from
our original three stations X, Y and Z, some from other stations.

Then arose the possibility of all sorts of confusion. The wrong line might be drawn. A report from Station X might be made to tally with a report from a station in the south of Ireland, and the point where the two lines met would be somewhere 100 miles out in the Atlantic – and there would be no U-boat there at all.

It was, therefore, necessary to find a means of isolating the calls, to discover which U-boat was talking, and which boat each station was reporting.

The British intelligence service owed a deep debt of gratitude to the Germans for their loyal adherence to method. The Germans had a plan, and they kept to it. No chopping or changing for them. There were no sudden or frequent alterations of system.

The U-boats always began their conversation by sending out their own secret code numbers. It was an invariable rule, and we thus came to know that the first letters of a call gave the code numeral of the submarine that was talking. This saved us a great deal of trouble.

When the intelligence officer at the base received simultaneously six reports from different stations, he looked at once for the first letters of each message. Three of the messages would begin with (let us say) MON. Three would begin with LRT.

And at once he had – again within a circle of 2 miles' radius – knowledge of the whereabouts of those two U-boats.

This sort of information, of course, was not intended merely for the entertainment of the shore staff, nor for the compilation of pretty dossiers to be filed in the Base Office.

It was passed at once to the senior naval officers concerned, for them to take the necessary steps to direct the patrols and the convoys that were in the path of the enemy.

Meantime the base intelligence officer (BIO) would turn to

the large-scale chart on the wall of his office and stick a pin with a coloured flag in the place where the U-boat was assumed to be.

Those flags represented not only the U-boats of which his own directional wireless stations (and other sources) had given him news; the chart covered a wide sweep of the seas, and showed the sections that were the immediate concern of neighbouring BIOs, as well as that under the control of his own base. They used the same flags as he did. It was not unlike the plan of working a railway, where one signal-box passes a train to the next. The U-boats were invisibly shadowed the whole time they were at sea, and signalled from one section to the next.

Sometimes the chart would simply bristle with pins. At other times there would be very few pins. This was because the intensity of the U-boat campaign was subject to violent fluctuations. The Germans were not always able to keep up the pressure.

The busiest month of all was June 1917. During that month the first of the big U-cruisers put to sea. There were twenty-seven boats of all types working in the North Sea and the Atlantic, thirteen in the Channel, fifteen in the Mediterranean, three in the Baltic, and two in the Black Sea. Yet in November of the same year the number of boats at sea had shrunk to thirty, while some thirty-five were located at various dockyards undergoing overhaul.

Anti-submarine intelligence work was not confined to such material facts as the position of the enemy. It was also very important to know the personal characteristics of the men in command. No two submarine commanders possessed the same skill, or the same courage, or pursued the same tactics. And our methods of dealing with them varied according to their characteristics. One man, known to be a dangerous and skilful opponent, would be tackled and trailed from the moment he was located. Another man, known to be a braggart, who fired torpedoes haphazard and returned home claiming to have sunk tens of thousands of tonnes of shipping – when his total bag was really one small sailing ship, holed but not sunk – could be safely left alone if he was not near any of our shipping lanes. It is a rather remarkable fact, which few except those who were closely engaged in anti-submarine work have ever realised, that only two out of the twenty best German submarine officers were killed during the war, and both lost their lives, not in action, but by their submarines hitting mines and blowing up.

Lieut-Commander Arnauld de la Perière, the most successful of all the U-boat captains, sank 400,000 tonnes of shipping, and Lieut-Commander Walther Forstmann was only 20,000 tonnes behind him. Whenever we picked up the trail of any submarine 'ace', the patrols and the Q-ships were specially warned.

These differences between the characteristics of the U-boat commanders were considered to be so important that each was represented on the wall chart by a different flag.

Thus, to go back to our imaginary pair, whose positions we noted from directional wireless reports a few pages back, MON would perhaps have a white flag with one black star on it, while LRT would be a black flag with a white line running across it diagonally. Everybody in the base intelligence office who had access to the anti-submarine room was thus presented with a clear picture of the position at sea from hour to hour. When further reports of the movements of those two submarines came in, an extra flag of each kind would be put on the chart to mark the new positions, and so we were able to trace the course the U-boat commander was steering and to obtain some idea of his objective – whether he was making for the Irish Sea to attack the Liverpool traffic, or whether he was on his way to the Atlantic and the Queenstown area.

In the same way, at Queenstown, they would be able to judge whether he was prowling in the Chops of the Channel, or whether he was aiming to work further south in the Bay of Biscay. In the latter event the Allied bases on the Biscayan coast would be able to pick him up and shadow him until he started on his way home again, when he would again be watched through the Queenstown area, and so up the Irish coast into the Scottish region, and round by the extreme north.

It is important here to point out that, though we kept this close watch on the movements of the submarine, our knowledge of its position was always approximate. Sometimes, of course, it was possible to get patrol ships to the spot very quickly and to harry the submarine, but the Atlantic is a very wide ocean, and more often than not the submarine's position was miles and miles away from our nearest ships.

Let us recall a typical scene in the base intelligence office at an important centre.

It was Sunday morning. Things were quiet. The wall chart had all the midnight positions of the U-boats marked up. It had nearly all their 8 a.m. positions, too. There was one that was missing, however. Nothing had been heard of him since midnight.

His various flags on the chart showed him to be steering southwards, and he had just reached the point where it was important for us to know whether he was going on south to the Bay of Biscay and the Spanish coast, or whether he would turn eastwards and worry us off the mouth of the Channel. There were patrolling destroyers on his line of route. They might sight him, if they were lucky, but it was more likely that the first news we should get of him would be an attack on some merchant ship, perhaps within 20 miles of where we were sitting ashore.

Some U-boat commanders were full of guile, and it was no uncommon occurrence for us to lose touch with them for two or three days on end. One of these 'dog foxes', whose pin had been stationary on the wall chart for some time, had not been using his wireless. He might be in trouble, or he might be preparing trouble. Watching U-boats, as the reader will have gathered by this time, involved much guessing and a great deal of patient waiting.

It was very quiet in the office. A clerk was silently docketing information at a little desk in the corner. The base intelligence officer, leaning back in his swing chair, was smoking his pipe, waiting with that indomitable patience that intelligence men learn to cultivate. The visitor stood before the wall chart, studying the whole position – which was new to him, since he had only arrived the previous night – weighing up the various factors, and mentally digesting the information that had been given to him.

The hands of the clock pointed to eleven when the green baize door swung quickly inwards, and a messenger came in.

He handed an official form to the BIO.

The ticking of the clock was the only sound for several seconds, while the officer read the message slowly through.

'Forty-seven twenty. Ten-ten,' he said at last.

The visitor glanced round at the first word, and then turned back again to the chart.

'He's off to Spain, then?' he suggested, having fixed the latitude and longitude that the figures indicated.

The BIO frowned, doubtfully.

'May be', he grunted. 'At the present moment he's pump-
ing shell into a Q-ship, and the poor devils in her are having a
pretty thin time of it.'

There was a moment of tense drama! The two men sitting in
safety in a cosy office on a peaceful Sabbath morning – the distant church bells had hardly ceased pealing – were discussing
the martyrdom of some forty or fifty brave fellows who had challenged death in order to deal out death by stratagem. They were
hundreds of miles away from that office, but the office knew all
about them – and in the corner of the war with which the office
was concerned even the death of those men would have been
but a mere incident.

The business of the office was to acquire knowledge of the
assailant. It was for others to send to the Q-ship's succour.

The BIO walked over to the wall chart and stood beside the
visitor, deep in thought.

'It must be him,' he said, half to himself, gazing at the little
rows of flags pinned one behind the other. 'None of the others
could have reached that position.'

He stretched out his hand and selected a flag from a tray. It
was black, with a white skull in the centre. He stuck it in the chart
at 47.2 N. 3.13 W. and put the telegram on a spike on his desk.

It was all he could do for the moment. There would be more
news later – perhaps. He returned to his task of waiting.

In a quarter of an hour another message came in.

The Q-ship had thrown off her disguise, after twenty minutes
of inferno, when the U-boat was lying about 400 yards away from
her on the surface. The Q-ship's gunners had loosed off half a
dozen rounds from each gun before the submarine went under
water. The captain of the mystery ship considered she was sunk.

The BIO read the message over, aloud.

'Optimist!' was his comment. 'No word of survivors or of wreckage. Still, it may have scared them a bit. We'll log it as possibly slightly damaged. I wish they had sent her number.'

The comment was typical.

Facts were the vital food of the intelligence officer. He did not want guesses or suppositions. He spent half his time rejecting theories because there were no facts to support them.

And that desire to know the U-boat's number had a two-fold origin. In the first place, it would have settled the correctness or otherwise of the previous night's decoding of the secret letters with which the wireless talk had started. In the second place, it would have enabled the base to be sure which of the enemy submarines was in that area. As matters stood, there was just a possibility that the attack had been delivered by a U-boat on its way home from the south – a newcomer, that is to say, in the area, who would have to be tracked all the time he was moving through our particular stretch of waters.

The first of these reasons was infinitely the more important from the intelligence officer's point of view. On the accuracy with which he decoded the secret call sign depended the accuracy of all his other information.

How was that decoding done?

There were dozens of different ways, of course, some of them still too confidential to be divulged even after this lapse of time. But a few of the more simple methods may be explained.

As is described above, our wireless directional stations would pick up the actual lettering of the message, and we knew, after long experience, that the first three or four letters gave the code number.

Let us, for the sake of simplicity, continue to use the two instances already quoted: one U-boat's call was MON; the other's was LRT.

With the help of the directional wireless bearings we had found the position of those two vessels on the chart. But our Base Office was a long way away from those positions. We wanted someone nearer the danger zone to discover certain facts for us. Who was available? Only time would tell us. We must wait for data as to the activity of each of the submarines.

MON at dawn sighted a small tramp steamer whose crew took to their boats. The U-boat came alongside to find out what the ship was, and perhaps to take the captain prisoner.

The keen-eyed mate spotted on the conning-tower, beneath the fresh layer of light-grey paint, the outline of letters and a number that looked like *U-99*, let us say. He bore it in mind, and when, some hours later, the drifting boats were picked up, he reported the fact to the commanding officer of the rescuing destroyer or patrol boat.

So the news would be passed on that the SS *War Baby* (to take an imaginary name) had been sunk in such and such a latitude, such and such a longitude, by a U-boat, supposed to be *U-99*.

In due course that news reached the base intelligence officer.

The position given agreed with the wireless directional placing of MON.

Therefore, until disproved, MON – *U-99*.

Five days later MON, now operating off the south coast of Ireland, sinks another steamer, and one of her crew, taunting the drifting survivors, shouts: 'Britain shall tremble at the name of *U-99*!'

The survivors are rescued and report the boastful threat.

And so, scrap by scrap, evidence piles up and proves our equation for us.

It must not be imagined that it was always as simple as in this particular case. For one thing, there might be no survivors. Once, when news was very urgently required for the purpose of establishing the identity of two submarines, one of them launched an attack. Five men got away from the sinking ship, on a raft. Several days later two of them, alive but unconscious, were picked up by a British submarine that happened, quite by chance, to sight the raft. Neither of the men was in a condition to give any information for a long time, and by then the tangle had been unravelled by other means.

Let us take the case of the identification of U-boat LRT. This case is a little different from that of MON.

Her commander is a 'dog fox' who never shows himself. He does his work with the torpedo. We only know that LRT is a code number that we would like to decode.

Then, suddenly, one day, we get a message from an intelligence agent in a neutral port. He has learned that a small sailing ship is putting out at night, and that local German emissaries have persuaded the skipper to take a few fresh provisions and their stores to a certain rendezvous, for delivery to the captain of *U-100*.

We go to the chart and scan the seas around that neutral port.

What U-boats are known to be working in that area? There is ADF about 150 miles away, but we know beyond all doubt that his number is *UB-80*.

Two hundred miles away is our last recorded position for LRT. He has been absent from his base more than a fortnight. Fresh provisions would be very welcome.

We begin to suspect that LRT = *U-100*.

That was how the work went on all through the war – slow, patient, plodding; pulling perhaps fifty wires in five different countries to extract one definite fact.

It will be realised that this was not 'spying' in the melodramatic sense at all. Indeed, only a man with a real imaginative sense (what the American business man calls a 'visualiser') would have seen the drama in the work. It was sheer intelligence, the using of one's wits to deduce the right conclusion from a given set of facts, with, perhaps, one vital clue missing. Those vital clues, too, had the oddest way of turning up from the most unexpected sources. Few people realised the need for a rigid censorship of the press. Intelligence men did. They found so often one little ray of light in an obscure paragraph in some provincial German paper, one tiny ultimate fact that linked up all the other information and completed a perfect jigsaw puzzle.

Sometimes that happened even with the tracking of submarines in the Atlantic, incredible as such a thing may seem to those who have never had to build up a case on scanty information.

There came a time when we had the secret code call of every German submarine deciphered and logged. They were all set out neatly in order, beginning at *U-5* – we never found any trace of the four earliest boats putting to sea during the war – and going right down through the *UB* and *UC* types to the last completed vessel in each class.

Not one of them could send a wireless message without letting us know exactly who was talking and whereabouts he lay.

'Ah!' exclaims the intelligent reader at this point; 'that is all very well: but codes are not like the laws of the Medes and Persians. They can be changed.'

In the intelligence department we said the same thing, at first. We knew that the British Navy had a challenge and reply code for each day, and that it was altered frequently. Surely the Germans did likewise.

We were on the alert for changes. Because MON stood for *U-99* on her first trip out, we did not, six weeks later, take it for granted that MON still equalled *U-99*. We looked for fresh evidence.

And, to our astonishment, we learned gradually that the secret U-boat call signs did not alter. They remained the same month after month. Apparently the highly organised German system was such that it would not bear change. We could vary our wireless code calls from day to day if we wanted to, without any disorganisation. The Germans, for some reason, were unable, or unwilling, to make any variation in theirs.

Then, after many months, and almost in the last phase of the war, we were suddenly confronted by a conflict of evidence about MON. He was out in the Atlantic, and had been sighted at close quarters on the surface by a destroyer. A rift in the clouds flooded the scene with moonlight, and on the conning-tower there showed up the number – *UB-17*.

At the same time other calls that we had not had before began to come in from the wireless directional stations.

The Germans had changed their code system at last.

All our lists of U-boat numbers were promptly scrapped. We forgot all that we had done and started afresh. Those were pretty strenuous days in the base intelligence offices and in the ID at Whitehall. It was a race against time to get out a new list that should be complete, with not a single number missing, and not one doubtful.

The methods were the same as before, perfected by practice.

Three weeks after we had detected the change, the whole of the work was done. Every new call was decoded and fixed to its proper submarine!

CHAPTER 14

ADVENTURES IN
COUNTER-ESPIONAGE

T HE ONLY WIDELY known 'fact' about British methods of counter-espionage and the watch that was kept on German intelligence agents in this country seems to be that, twenty-four hours before the outbreak of war, all the German emissaries in Britain were rounded up and put under lock and key.

That is true enough, as far as it goes, but it is only a tiny fragment of the story. Counter-espionage went on all through the war, not only in Great Britain, but also in every neutral country. The German secret service, finding it extraordinarily difficult to place agents in this country during the war, was largely dependent on the services of neutrals. Moreover, the seas being closed to Germany's shipping and all but closed to her men-of-war, it became necessary for the Berlin naval command to create in neutral ports supply and urgent repair bases for their submarines.

It was part of our naval intelligence duties to watch those activities, and wherever possible to circumvent them. This was one of the most difficult tasks of the war. It was full of peril, both to life and liberty. A number of the men engaged in it 'disappeared' without trace, and those who escaped the assassin's knife or bullet were in constant danger of overstepping the limits that any neutral government could be expected to stand, and thus finding themselves in a foreign prison, without any hope of aid from the British consul or ambassador.

Rounding up the German agents in Britain on the eve of the war was comparatively easy, because all of them had been known to a certain department for about three years and kept under constant surveillance.

This was officially disclosed in a Home Office statement, published on 8 October 1914. The statement was as follows:

> *In view of the anxiety naturally felt by the public with regard to the system of espionage on which Germany has placed so much reliance, it may be well to state briefly the steps that the Home Office, acting on behalf of the admiralty and War Office, has taken to deal with the matter in this country. The secrecy that it has hitherto been desirable, in the public interest, to observe on certain points cannot any longer be maintained, owing to the evidence that it is necessary to produce in cases against spies now pending.*
>
> *It was clearly ascertained five or six years ago (i.e. 1909–10) that the Germans were making great efforts to establish a system of espionage in this country, and in order to trace and thwart these efforts a special intelligence department was established*

by the admiralty and the War Office, which has ever since acted in the closest cooperation with the Home Office and the Metropolitan Police, and the principal provincial police forces. In 1911, by passing of the Official Secrets Act, the law with regard to espionage, which had hitherto been confused and defective, was put on a clear basis, and extended so as to embrace every possible mode of obtaining and conveying to the enemy information that might be useful in war.

The special intelligence department, supported by all the means that could be placed at its disposal by the Home Secretary, was able in three years, from 1911 to 1914, to discover the ramifications of the German secret service in England. In spite of enormous efforts and lavish expenditure of money by the enemy, little valuable information passed into their hands. The agents, of whose identity knowledge was obtained by the special intelligence department, were watched and shadowed without, in general (the department), taking any hostile action, or allowing them to know that their movements were watched.

When, however, any actual step was taken to convey plans or documents of importance from this country to Germany, the spy was arrested, and in such case evidence sufficient to secure his conviction was usually found in his possession. Proceedings were taken under the Official Secrets Act by the director of public prosecutions, and in six cases sentences were passed varying from eighteen months' to six years' penal servitude.

At the same time steps were taken to mark down and keep under observation all the agents known to be engaged in this traffic, so that when any necessity arose the police might lay hands on them at once, and accordingly on 4 August, before the declaration of war, instructions were given by the Home Secretary for the arrest

*of twenty known spies, and all were arrested. This figure does not
cover a large number (upwards of 200) who were noted as under
suspicion or to be kept under special observation.*

*The great majority of these were interned at, or soon after, the
declaration of war.*

It is fairly certain that the names of some of our intelligence men
were also known to the Germans. The outbreak of the war found
several of these men still in central Europe, and although most of
them received a code warning in time to make their exit to neutral
countries, there were some exceptions. These included one or two
really brilliant men, of whose fate we know nothing to this day.

The British security service had two extraordinary pieces of
luck in its pre-war work of tracing the men who were working
here for Germany.

During 1911 a British intelligence agent home on leave was
making a cycling tour with a friend, and they put up for a night
or two at a hotel in an East Coast port. As it was a naval base as
well as a commercial port, and holiday resorts were quite near
at hand, it was precisely the sort of place in which confidential
information might be picked up. But the ID man had no idea of
doing any counter-espionage when he went there. The opportunity came his way by pure chance.

The hotel manager, apparently British-born, was a friendly
sort of person, full of good stories. One night, for some unknown
reason, he chose to 'celebrate' in company with the two cyclists,
inviting them into his private office to keep up the jollification
after the business of the day was done.

The wine loosened his tongue, though it had no effect on the
purity of his English accent, and he became expansive.

The ID man, reconstructing the scene for a subsequent report, described it in these words:

As far as can be remembered the following is a verbatim report of his unsolicited admissions:

'It is rather amusing to think that I, a German ex-soldier and a former private in the British infantry, who also know a good deal about naval matters through having two brothers who are Deckoffiziere *(warrant officers) in the German Navy, should be holding the position I do. I know all about the strength and composition of the British naval forces in this part of the world, and, thanks to my many acquaintances among the NCO's and men of the local garrison, I have a perfect knowledge of all the harbour defences and battery positions within this area. Wouldn't I be a useful man to the Germans if war ever comes?'*

After expressing mild surprise and interest at these disclosures, the two auditors put a few leading questions, which the man's natural vanity and his bibulous state led him to answer. He even went to the length of admitting that he had already been in communication with certain authorities in Germany, from whom he had received instructions as to his procedure in the event of strained relations developing between Great Britain and Germany.

In other words, that English-speaking hotel manager was a self-confessed German agent of a really dangerous type, planted in the midst of a vital area in the British East Coast defences, and he had practically boasted of the fact to one of our ID men! It need hardly be said that thereafter he was kept under strict surveillance, though so unobtrusively that he never suspected it, and at the outbreak of war he was one of the twenty enemy agents who went into prison.

For three years previously his correspondence had been subjected to close scrutiny. One of his letters, which really did contain vital information, was so skilfully 'touched up' before it left England that its purport must have conveyed an utterly erroneous impression to the addressees in Berlin.

His accommodation address in Newcastle-on-Tyne was discovered in less than a week after he had committed his blazing indiscretion.

The clue that led right to the heart of the German secret service in Britain was due to another indiscretion, which had not even the excuse of being committed under the influence of drink. Regarded from any angle, it was an unpardonable piece of folly.

Among the members of the Kaiser's suite on one of his visits to England was an officer holding a very high position in the German Admiralty. He was known by the British security service to be keenly interested in the work of the German secret service, but they hardly supposed that he would take any active part in such work while he was in England. More as a matter of routine than for any definite purpose, his movements were unobtrusively shadowed.

Late one evening he left the house in which he was quartered in London, wearing mufti, and drove away. The car was followed, though it seemed quite likely that he was only bound for some official reception or dance.

To the surprise of the shadower, the car drove on into the suburbs, and one of the poorer suburbs, of north London. It stopped outside a small shop, already closed for the night; but the visitor was evidently expected, for the side door opened as soon as the car stopped, and he went straight in without knocking.

He stayed a considerable time, and, on coming out, got into the car quickly and was driven back to his quarters.

This shop, at 402a, Caledonian Road, was not known to the civil police authorities to be a cloak for any illicit business, so the security people took the matter in hand.

The man who kept the shop, one Karl Gustav Ernst, was soon found to be the clearing agent for the reports of more than half the men working in England for the German secret service. (It was revealed in the subsequent proceedings against him that he had been paid the munificent salary of £1 a month by the German secret service!) Thereafter all his correspondence was watched until the war broke out, when he was arrested.

It was a remarkable fact that, before the war, intelligence men in all countries used the post with the utmost freedom, trusting to luck, presumably, that no suspicion attached to them. Little more organisation, and little more expense, would have been needed to institute a service of couriers carrying the letters on their travels to and from neutral countries, where the correspondence would not have been subject to surveillance. As soon as the war began, the Germans did start to try to build up such a service from England to Holland, and there must be quite a number of perfectly honest and innocent Dutch business men who still remember the severity with which they were examined and cross-examined every time they entered or left Harwich.

Those who were couriers for the German intelligence department became very astute at hiding incriminating documents in order to smuggle them through. One man whom it took us a long time to catch with the evidence on him became so accustomed to being searched that he once said, jokingly, to the searchers at

Harwich that he automatically began to take his clothes off as the train slowed up at the platform, and before he left the carriage!

The way we got him in the end was rather neat. The ID knew for a fact that he had been in touch with a suspect here, from whom he had received some information that must be put on paper. It could not possibly have been memorised. Therefore, somewhere on his person that writing was concealed.

He went into the search room at Harwich with the usual smile on his face. Sitting at the table was a strange officer, of senior rank, watching the search, but taking no part in it. All the usual tests were applied – false heels, false soles, hiding places in the lining of the hat, and so on. Nothing was found. All this time the strange officer had not said a word. He just watched.

The searchers seemed to be beaten. The chief man scratched his head, and looked round in amused bewilderment at the officer.

The latter rapped out a brusque order.

'Take out your false teeth!'

The courier made a movement of protest.

'Out with them!'

The head of the search-party had an inspiration. 'Seize his arms,' he shouted, before the courier could put hand to mouth. Then the searcher gently forced the mouth open, took out the top denture, and from the roof of the man's mouth a tiny packet of oiled silk, not the thickness of a postage stamp, fell on his tongue. Inside the packet was the information in microscopic writing.

Those who had to travel abroad during the war were often puzzled by the regulation that no newspapers or books should be taken out of the country. Although this rule was enforced more rigidly in France than here, we frequently put it into operation ourselves. The reason was that information of which the printer and the publisher knew nothing could still be conveyed by the printed page. A pinprick alongside certain selected words could be 'read' by those in the secret, and the pricked words would make up a complete message.

Invisible inks and other tricks of that sort were, of course, child's play to the security service. We knew them all long before the war, and as a matter of fact no competent intelligence man in any service ever relied on them. Codes were a different matter. It is fairly well known now that a certain type of mind has a genius for evolving and solving cryptograms. Sir Alfred Ewing, the director of naval education, possessed such a mind, and he has publicly told the story of 'Room 40', where he and a staff of similarly gifted assistants grappled with the problems of codes all through the war.

He disclosed the secret in a speech before the Edinburgh Philosophical Institution in December 1927.

He said that in 1914 he was director of naval education at the admiralty. On the day war was declared he was asked to undertake the task of dealing with enemy ciphers. That was the beginning of what grew to be an important organisation for collecting and deciphering enemy messages.

He enlisted a few friends to come in and help: they worked hard and had remarkable luck, so that the deciphering staff was soon established as a separate branch of the admiralty under his direction. Numerous listening stations were set up.

'In that way,' Sir Alfred said,

A close and constant watch was kept on the German fleet. The branch of the admiralty where this was done was called Room 40, to avoid any description that might betray the secret or excite

curiosity. The fact that such work was going on was known to very
few persons, even in official circles or in the fleet. It remained a
secret to the end, and was probably the best-kept secret of the war.

Sir Alfred Ewing also referred to the fact that we took in Schwieger's triumphant message from *U-20* announcing the sinking of the *Lusitania*.

'Besides intercepting naval signals,' he added, 'the cryptographers dealt successfully with much cipher to Germany's agents in Madrid, North and South America, Constantinople, Athens, Sofia, and other places. One group of deciphered messages threw useful light in advance on the Easter Rebellion in Ireland, and another on the German intrigues in Persia.

Among the many political messages read by the staff was the notori-
ous Zimmermann telegram, which revealed a conditional offer to
Mexico of an alliance against the United States. President Wilson
was then hesitating on the brink of war, reluctant to plunge, cling-
ing painfully to the idea of neutrality, which seemed almost part of
his religion. The message was communicated, very confidentially,
by Lord Balfour to Mr Page (the US ambassador), and through
Mr Page to President Wilson, who gave it to the American press.

During the war our efforts to decipher enemy codes were facilitated by captures from German ships. The first piece of luck came our way when the German cruiser *Magdeburg* ran ashore in fog on the island of Odenholm in the Baltic. She had to be abandoned by her crew, and measures were taken to blow her up. But, for some inexplicable reason, her confidential books, including signal books and ciphers, were not destroyed. This could not have been overlooked in the haste of abandoning ship, for the *Magdeburg's* captain, Commander Habenicht, declined to leave the ship, and was captured by the Russians.

Anyway, the code books fell into the hands of the Russians, who promptly communicated their contents to the British Admiralty, thus enabling us, for some time at any rate, to decode German wireless messages without any trouble.

German submarines now and again sank in water shallow enough to allow of salvage operations. In their case the possibility of destroying the confidential books was small, as will be realised, and from the wrecked hulls we now and again extracted useful papers. *UC-44* was a case in point.

So far as naval intelligence work was concerned, the last three years of the war were almost exclusively concerned with the submarine campaign. Tracking the U-boats was the province of the base intelligence office, but there was also work for men who operated less officially in neutral countries, keeping track of the German agents who were working in the neutral ports to assist the U-boats.

Presumably by this time the venerable legend about secret dumps of petrol is dead, but, lest it should still survive, let us put on record here that all the German submarines from *U-19* onwards were driven by heavy-oil engines, the German Admiralty having obtained as far back as 1911 a satisfactory four-stroke engine from the Augsburg works.

True, the earlier U-boats had Körting engines driven by petrol, but they were soon in a minority in the fleet, and were always disliked on account of the fumes that revealed their presence. Indeed, Spiess says of *U-9* that her exhaust pipes glittered with sparks, and even with flames, which betrayed her presence at night. Moreover, so far as cruising endurance was concerned, these petrol boats in the winter of 1912–13 had stayed at sea alone for eleven days, without mother ships or fuel ships. So there was never the slightest need for hoards of petrol, in two-gallon tins, in secret islands or lonely coves on neutral shores, for the use of the U-boat captain. And since a moderate-sized submarine carries anything from 50 to 75 tonnes of heavy oil, it will be obvious that a dump of half a dozen barrels would not be any great help. It may be taken as a fact that no secret hoards of petrol for German submarines ever existed: consequently our intelligence officers had no adventures in looking for them.

Von Tirpitz seemed to be under the impression that such secret bases were suspected, and that his agent in Sardinia was interned because he was supposed to be running such a base. But the reason for that gentleman's internment had nothing to do with petrol. (In the course of the extravagant proceedings in the Aegean and the wild-cat adventures of the self-styled 'secret service men' who were let loose on that unhappy area, certain stories about U-boat petrol bases appear to have been circulated – perhaps fomented would be the better word. They were unworthy of the inventive ability of any novelist, and a poor testimony to the professional knowledge of the foreign naval officer concerned in the propaganda.)

On the other hand, supplies of spare parts to replace damaged machinery became indispensable as the U-boats' radius of action increased. A boat damaged somewhere in the south of the Bay of Biscay, and consequently unable to dive, could hardly hope to get back to her base in the Bight of Heligoland. Repairs had to be effected somehow. Under international law a warship in need of repairs to make her seaworthy may shelter in a neutral port for twenty-four hours, but no longer. This meant that an efficient shore staff had to be available to lend a hand in getting the work done, and the maintenance of a fairly wide range of spares for any emergency.

We knew where all these repair depots were situated just as well as the U-boat captains, and we, too, had an efficient shore staff ready to lend a hand – to prevent the repairs from being made.

Here is one typical case.

A U-boat operating well out in the Atlantic had a breakdown in the engine room. While the damage was not fatal, it was crippling to her activity, especially if she were harassed by enemy craft and compelled to keep down for too long. The captain and the crew both knew, from experience, what they would have to face on the long journey back, and they could not afford to make too wide a detour, lest the supply of oil fuel ran out. Their expenditure had been calculated to a nicety.

Consequently, unless repairs could be effected the outlook was gloomy. So the submarine stood in towards the neutral coast and wirelessed her needs to the local German agent. The submarine expert on the spot knew exactly what was wanted, but he had not got that particular spare part in stock. Nor could he procure it anywhere in the port. It would have to be sent from another German depot in another part of the country.

It was useless for the submarine to come in under the plea of stress of circumstances unless the repair could be carried out within twenty-four hours. So, after much wireless conversation, it was arranged that the U-boat should remain off shore for a few days until the required parts could be obtained.

All this time our intelligence men in the port were on the

watch. They knew something of what was toward, and they guessed most of the rest. Their essential task was to keep in touch with the German submarine expert ashore and to learn what he was doing. By means that need not be detailed, this was soon known to us. The problem then before us was how to trap the submarine.

Two days later the German submarine came into harbour, where her captain formally applied for permission to remain twenty-four hours, to effect the repairs necessary to make her seaworthy. He was rather surprised at the coldness of his reception. The local authorities had a reputation for being pro-German, or so the German agents had always reported. What he did not know was that the chief of the port had received very urgent instructions from headquarters, forbidding on this occasion any deviation from the strict rule. And those instructions had been originated by diplomatic pressure from the British side.

There was perturbation at the German headquarters at this development, for the submarine commander had come into harbour twelve hours earlier than they had expected him. In point of fact his crew had got more than a little nervous at remaining in the same area so long, for they quite expected to be attacked by some of the Allied patrol craft, or possibly blockaded in the neutral port.

What had happened was that the German repair party had arranged for the wanted parts to arrive that afternoon by train, and they had not looked for the submarine until next day. It was going to be a strenuous business to get the work done, even if the train came in punctually.

Actually, it arrived two hours late. Then there was a great scurrying of the German agents to get their goods unloaded.

They had previously used a great deal of palm oil to facilitate matters.

But the vans with the precious parts were not on the train!

The air was thick with guttural curses as the Germans tore frantically up and down the train, cross-examining employees of the railway. The head of the British intelligence branch in the port, who happened to be passing that way – quite by chance, of course – smiled to see the commotion, and went back to his office quite satisfied with his after-lunch stroll.

It was a most hectic afternoon for the Germans. They made telephone inquiries all up and down the line, but could not trace the missing wagons. These had apparently vanished into thin air.

A very crestfallen group sat in conference on board the U-boat that night. It was impossible to replace the missing fittings within the fifteen hours that remained. The crew could not face the trip home without the security of being able to dive and stay under when emergency arose.

In the end the U-boat captain went to the port commander and told him that, as the repairs could not be completed within the specified twenty-four hours, he would have to offer himself and his boat for internment. And interned they stayed for the rest of the war.

What had become of the missing wagons?

It was quite simple. Knowing as we did what the wagons would contain, it was necessary to see that they did not arrive. So, while the train was being made up in the goods yard of the town from which the parts were being despatched, two British agents, with a thorough knowledge of the customs and regulations of that railway line, were working there. They found the two wagons – and rubbed out the destination marks they bore. Then they chalked other destination marks on the wagons, and those destinations were right away on the other side of the country.

The goods-yard superintendent in that distant port was puzzled at receiving two wagons that he knew nothing about. He shunted them into a siding, and then began a correspondence about them that may be going on to this day.

That same country, though not the same port, was the scene of another railway comedy.

In the tower of a house near the seaboard, the German secret service had a wireless installation that they used quite openly to communicate with their submarines. We repeatedly made formal protests to the local authorities, but without effect. There were many influential German sympathisers along that stretch of coast. The officials were quite polite to us, but they professed themselves unable to do anything. At last, however, we persuaded headquarters to move. The local people were peremptorily ordered by the government to dismantle this wireless station forthwith, in view of the evidence received as to its existence and purpose.

The Germans were quite unmoved by the decision. They had l aid their plans to meet just such an emergency. All they had to do was to despatch the entire equipment by train a little further along the coast, into another province where a fresh set of local authorities would be concerned – and the game would begin all over again.

But they had reckoned without the British intelligence service.

The wireless station was dismantled and the parts loaded on the train for despatch, according to plan. The train left the goods yard according to timetable. And that was the last ever seen of that German wireless equipment. As the train rumbled on through the night, two British agents who had hidden themselves on board broke open the crates and scattered the gear all along the lines, in the ditches and the fields and the ravines through which the railway ran.

It is to be feared that they also dealt in the same unceremonious way with the body of the German who was travelling in charge of the gear. When the need arose, secret service work was not conducted in kid gloves by either of the opposing parties.

That much is made evident by another story, this time from the United States.

Before America came into the war it was, of course, the business of her authorities to see that none of the interned German ships got away to act as a commerce destroyer. But we were able to give them a good deal of help in the work, owing to our specialised knowledge of the personnel and methods of the Teutonic war organisation 'behind the lines' in the United States.

Of the score or more of German liners that had voluntarily interned themselves in New York Harbour on the outbreak of the war, at least six proposed to get away if they could. Arrangements had been made by German agents for these vessels to meet, at a rendezvous off Virginia Capes; a camouflaged German ship would supply them with guns, ammunition and other requisites for their mission as commerce raiders.

In point of fact, none of those German ships ever did leave the Hudson River until they were impounded by the United States in 1917.

It is popularly supposed that the reason why this great fleet of German liners lay quiescent in American harbours for more than two and a half years was the presence of British cruisers off the North American coast. That those 'distant, storm-battered ships' of the King's Navy were partly responsible for the immobilisation of Germany's large potential fleet of commerce destroyers is indubitably a fact; but while the outer seas were held by our cruisers, there was an inner guard, invisible but unsleeping, which kept the imprisoned ships under constant observation.

It would have been perfectly easy for any one of those liners to get to sea at night or during foggy weather, but for several inhibitive factors.

In the first place, the amount of fuel in the bunkers of each vessel was known to the British intelligence service, and had any German ship attempted to replenish its fuel supply, the news would have reached our headquarters within a few hours.

The disclosure may now be made that persons in the employ of the British intelligence service were stationed at every port on the Atlantic coast of the United States, from Portland, Maine, to the Gulf, and that, in consequence, no enemy ship could even prepare for a move without a warning being almost instantly conveyed to British headquarters.

Many of the people who kept watch and ward at those ports were humble individuals who performed a very dangerous duty from purely patriotic motives. One person who was responsible for observing enemy shipping at a port not a hundred miles from New York was a working man. His despatches and memoranda sent to headquarters were models of terse English, reflecting the keenest powers of observation. For two and a half years he performed his duties admirably, though in constant danger from the machinations of the central European agents who swarmed in the eastern states.

Then, one morning, his body was found floating in the dock, riddled with bullets.

CHAPTER 15

THE LIGHTER SIDE OF ID WORK

A MIDST ALL THE hazards and vicissitudes of intelligence work there is a redeeming element of comedy.

Perhaps the greatest source of amusement for members of the ID during the war was the desperate solemnity of amateur spy-hunters. One and all meant to be most helpful. They were quite convinced that our security service was utterly incompetent. At times, indeed, some of them went so far as to declare that it must be staffed by enemy agents, so impervious did it remain to the 'information' laid before it by patriotic British citizens.

It was amusing, but it was also annoying, because, in the early days at least, information received had to be examined in case there was anything in it. The number of mares' nests that the security agents were invited to probe was almost past belief. Here is a typical case, every word of which is vouched for.

A certain person developed a craze for deciphering 'personal' advertisements in the daily papers. (And here it is but just to pay tribute to the patriotism of the daily papers, which went to the greatest possible pains to ensure that the advertisements accepted by them were genuine and harmless. Time and again they refused advertisements because they were not satisfied.)

The person in question used to bombard the naval intelligence department with cuttings from the personal column, with his own decoded version of what he thought the message really meant – and that was always, of course, some naval or military secret.

It was useless for us to write and tell him, as we did a dozen times or more, that we had made inquiries, and found that the message would not bear the interpretation he put on it, the advertisement being a perfectly genuine one. He simply did not believe us, and bombarded us with more.

At last the officer in charge of that department determined to see the man himself, and wrote, fixing an appointment.

When the visitor arrived he was so excited that he could hardly wait to get into the room before blurting out his latest discovery.

'Did you see this advertisement yesterday?' he demanded, thrusting a marked copy of the previous day's paper under the officer's nose. His thumb pointed to a small two-line notice, that ran, as far as memory recalls the exact wording, as follows: 'Ethel. Sorry I cannot meet you under the limes at five o'clock. – Sally.'

The head of the department solemnly read it through.

'Yes, I saw that,' he admitted.

'I have decoded it!' exclaimed his visitor, quivering with excitement. 'There is no doubt about it being a communication to the enemy. See, here is the real meaning of the message,' and he thrust a sheet of paper into the officer's hand.

On it was written: 'To all Channel U-boats. Two transports with troops leave Southampton eight o'clock tonight.'

The officer read through the decoding with a perfectly grave face.

'That is most interesting,' he said solemnly.

'I knew it! I knew it!' cried his visitor, almost dancing with joy. 'What have I always told you? Those messages are put in by German spies.'

The officer looked up at him with just a glimmer of a smile in his eye.

'Do you know…' he said, and paused dramatically, 'I inserted that advertisement myself, just to see what you would make of it?'

It was perfectly true, but the ingenious cryptographer refused to credit it, and probably believes to this day that the head of the department was trying to 'save face'.

But a moment's reflection will expose the absurdity of the visitor's theory. Let us assume that such a message had been inserted by an enemy agent, and that, when decoded, it did bear the meaning ascribed to it by the enthusiast for decoding. Of what value could it be to the enemy?

A paper published in London on, say, Monday morning, could not reach an enemy country for several days, and would not even get to any neutral country until Tuesday, at the earliest. Then the information had to be conveyed to the German naval command and relayed to the U-boats in the Channel – and by that time the transports would be either in a French harbour or well out in the Bay of Biscay.

In any case, the personal column was so obvious an object of suspicion that no astute enemy agent was ever likely to use it.

Far more probable was a code message hidden in an advertisement relating to a flat to be let or a cook-general wanted.

We soon found that out for ourselves, and quickly had under lock and key the only enemy agent, so far as is known, who had the wit to use this method of getting into touch with confederates. He wanted to communicate with a man in Glasgow to whom he dared not write, as he suspected (quite rightly) that the man's correspondence was being watched.

A really valuable source of information, during wartime, is the enemy prisoner, if he can be persuaded to talk. Very properly, all officers and men were warned by their own authorities not to answer any questions if they were captured. They must know nothing.

Most of the German naval prisoners we interrogated were taciturn. But sometimes they were more talkative, and on one occasion we wrung a most vital admission from a German officer by the suavest methods. The story is hardly known outside the ID, but it deserves a wider public.

It concerns a certain Lieutenant-Commander the Freiherr Spiegel von und zu Peckelsheim – which really is his name, and not one invented to heighten the humour of the story.

Now and again even our own naval intelligence department found some plausible piece of fiction a useful instrument for its purpose. This happened whenever we found the right kind of enemy agent on whom to plant a terminological inexactitude.

The Freiherr Spiegel, however, was unlucky. His lie came home to roost.

He was a U-boat commander who, in the early days of the

war, made a series of successful cruises, reaching the Atlantic by the north-about route, and the Channel through the Straits of Dover. Then he wrote a book on his exploits under the title *U-202*. Taken for all in all it was quite a good book, and in the main as accurate as it could be, considering that he had to avoid the disclosure of secrets. But in one chapter he went sadly astray. It was headed 'England's Respect for the Red Cross', and in it he described, with much virtuous indignation, how he had seen one of our hospital ships 'laden with guns right fore and aft, and an army of soldiers and horses was packed between the guns and their mountings'.

Both he and his second-in-command, he declared, saw all this through the periscope, and he had stamped his feet on the steel plating of the conning-tower until it rattled, in his rage at being unable, on account of the ship's distance and speed, to cut her off, and so to punish the 'mean hypocritical brutes'. That book appeared before the United States entered the war, and a translation of it was published serially in a number of American papers. Now, a statement of that sort was bound to do us harm. We knew it to be untrue. Never once did we use hospital ships for any purpose but the legitimate one of carrying sick and wounded. But a neutral could, if he liked, say that he had as much right to believe the word of a German as that of an Englishman.

It was the business of the naval intelligence department (NID) to nail Baron Spiegel's lie to the counter.

There were the intelligence men in the admiralty chained to their desks. There was the Baron still roaming the seas, or possibly transferred to training duty in a shore establishment where it was too much to hope that we could reach him. And yet we wanted him badly. A chat with him would probably put a very different complexion on that chapter in his book.

We had to get into touch with him somehow.

What we needed was a link, and since, as in most intelligence work, the forging of that link depended three parts on patience and one part on luck, the ID men did not fret.

They mentally pigeon-holed the name of the Freiherr Spiegel von und zu Peckelsheim, and addressed themselves to other tasks until such time as a turn of fortune's wheel brought him to the forefront again.

And all the time the link was quietly forging itself. It took the shape of a little 800-tonne topsail schooner, inoffensive and unpretentious. Our anti-submarine people took a fancy to her. She looked so harmless – and could so easily conceal a menace. In appearance she resembled a score of other small sailing ships that German submarines used as targets for their 4-inch guns when they met them in the Atlantic, off the Irish coast.

So this little schooner, the *Prize*, went into a dockyard for two or three weeks. She emerged outwardly the same, but actually a very different ship. She was still a sailing ship, but she now carried a hidden 4-inch gun, and her crew were ratings of the Royal Navy, while her captain was a Colonial fighter, Lieutenant William Edward Sanders, RNR, a man of whom New Zealand has reason to be proud.

The *Prize*, in short, had been converted into a Q-ship, one of the U-boat traps that caused much anxiety in German naval circles for some time.

She sailed into the Atlantic, steering on a course that conformed to the trade on which she was supposed to be engaged.

On the morning of 30 April 1917, she was attacked with gunfire by a large German submarine. The *Prize* was shelled for twenty minutes before the right moment came for her to throw off her disguise and retaliate. Her 'panic party' left her in the lifeboat, thus giving the impression that the ship had been abandoned. Those left hidden on board to work the concealed gun lay very still until the submarine, now on the surface, came quite near and offered a good mark. Then the screens went down and the gun was fired.

One shell demolished the U-boat's forward gun, and killed the crew. Another smashed the conning-tower, and three people were seen to fall into the water.

In four minutes the U-boat, shorn of her conning tower and with her deck buckled by shell fire, went under water.

Then the 'panic party' from the *Prize* pulled to the spot in their boat and picked up the three men who had been blown overboard.

Here let us, in the manner of the cinema, switch off quickly and throw another picture on the screen – an office in the admiralty, a senior officer busy at his desk. To him there enters another officer, with a naval telegraph form. We will throw it on the screen thus:

HMS Prize *engaged and believed sank*
U-93, *latitude-longitude-yesterday.*
Three survivors.

The two officers look at each other quickly and both utter the same words simultaneously: 'Spiegel von Peckelsheim.'

For they knew the names of practically all the officers in command of U-boats.

Was the Baron one of the three survivors?

And the cinema switches back to the deck of the *Prize*, where Lieut Sanders is receiving his prisoners.

One is an ordinary seaman.

One is a warrant officer.

And the third, from his uniform, is an officer of the rank of lieutenant-commander. He presents himself and gives his name. Sanders is no linguist, and the guttural noises mean little to him. He merely asks his prisoners if they will give their parole not to interfere with the working of the ship.

The German officer goes further than this. He sees that the *Prize* is in a sinking condition. His gunnery had been pretty effective in those hectic twenty minutes.

He offers to help in plugging the holes and manning the pumps.

So victors and vanquished, 120 miles from land, with never a ship in sight, set to work together to encompass their earthly salvation. They sailed that water-logged colander of a ship 115 miles before they were picked up and towed into harbour by a patrol ship.

Meanwhile the NID waited patiently for further news. A telegram had been sent to the base requesting the full names of the survivors, and in due course these came to hand. The first was Lieutenant-Commander Freiherr Spiegel von und zu Peckelsheim.

So the officer who was particularly interested in the Baron took from a drawer in his desk a copy of the book *U-202* and, with red ink, underlined certain phrases in the chapter about the hospital ships. Then he gave the necessary orders for the disposal of the prisoners – and quietly returned to his other work. In two days he would confront his man.

It was a large room, hung with charts and a few naval pictures. The big fireplace was enclosed by a club fender, and on the mantelpiece stood a box of cigars. There was in one corner of the room a large pedestal desk; behind it were two great safes in which were locked half the secrets of the war at sea.

Under the desk on most days there lay a big, handsome black chow, the officer's inseparable companion. In another corner there stood, of all queer objects, a motor scooter. The indefatigable officer used this in order to get quickly from his home to the office in the middle of the night if he happened to be wanted. It saved the five minutes necessary for getting the car out of the garage.

Two high windows looked out over the wide open space of the Horse Guards Parade. A few easy chairs and a deep sofa stood here and there about the room.

It was into this setting that the Baron was introduced.

His host – and captor – was standing by the club fender. The German officer clicked his heels and gave a stiff, embarrassed bow. The host pulled a chair towards the fireplace.

'Won't you sit down?' he said silkily. He was as smooth as a kid glove.

The Baron obeyed. He even took the cigar that was offered to him. No doubt he saw in these preliminaries an attempt to bring him into the right mood for giving away German naval secrets, and, quite naturally, he determined to be especially discreet. He was very much on his guard against everything except that which really happened.

The British officer suddenly held up in front of him a copy of *U-202*.

'You know that book, I think,' he said.

235

The German stammered an affirmative. He was palpably disconcerted.

'I was very much interested in it,' the British officer continued quietly. 'Of course, you were very discreet in writing it. It doesn't tell us much that we didn't know – except in one chapter, and it was about that one that I wanted to see you.'

Smiling amiably at his victim, he looked a very harmless and incompetent elderly gentleman. The German relaxed his tension somewhat.

The British officer turned over the pages, gazing at them through a pair of horn-rimmed spectacles.

'Ah, yes! Here it is!' he said at last. 'This chapter about the hospital ship with guns and troops on board. Now, do you know, we cannot trace that particular occasion. I wonder if you could help us?'

The German remained silent.

'You say you saw the incident yourself?'

The German nodded.

'When did you see it?' There was a shade more authority in the voice.

Silence.

'When and where did you see it? What was the date?'

There was something inexorable in the voice. The questions were hammered at the prisoner with an iron determination. The mild, elderly gentleman had been transformed into the stern mentor.

'It is here, in print, in your native tongue, in a book published under your name. Did you write it?'

'Yes.'

'Is it true or untrue?'

A pause. The German was breathing heavily.

'I did not see it myself.'

'Ah!' The interrogator picked him up quickly. 'Then your second-in-command, this Mr Gröning, saw it and reported it to you?'

'No,' the answer came reluctantly.

'Then why did you say it?'

'I was told it was so.'

'On that particular day?'

'No. On several occasions.'

'But, you never saw, with your own eyes, British hospital ships carrying troops and guns?'

There was a long, painful pause. The German stood up.

'I never did,' he said. 'I was told it was so.'

'You were told so by your propaganda department in order that you might include the lie in your book?'

But to that question the Baron returned no answer.

It was not really necessary. We had his confession that the whole story was fabricated. The conversation had been taken down verbatim by a concealed stenographer whose transcript was endorsed by hidden witnesses. We had no need of further evidence.

The facts were promptly issued to the press of the entire world.

There is an interesting pendant to this story.

U-93 was not sunk. Severely damaged though she was, she remained watertight, and managed to limp home and report the loss of her captain and the others who had fallen overboard. It was inquiries for these men through the Red Cross a few weeks later that told us the *Prize*'s gallant effort had not ended the career of that particular submarine. But it had not been fruitless, since it enabled us to clear our good name by the personal testimony of the man who had sought to tarnish it with a lie.

One would have supposed the hospital ship calumny to have been dead long ago, but ten years after the Armistice German writers on the naval campaign were still repeating it.

That particular British naval officer had a *flair* for dealing with suspicious people and enemy prisoners. He was a most versatile actor. He could be the polished, easy, rather lackadaisical man-of-the-world. He could be the kindly, well-meaning, nervous, friendly sort of person, incapable of hurting a fly. And, when the need arose, he could outdo any Prussian drill sergeant at the game of brutal browbeating. One of his triumphs was the trapping of a suspect who had successfully run the gauntlet of four of our other examiners.

This man, living in a certain neutral country, was, ostensibly, a citizen of another neutral country. We had long had our eye on him. We were as sure as we could be, without written proof, that he was not only a German agent, but a native-born German to boot. But there was nothing in the way he spoke the tongue of his adopted country to betray his origin, and he appeared to know no German.

For a while we kept him under close observation in that neutral country where he was carrying on an innocent and legitimate business, which we were convinced was a mere cloak. Then, acting on instructions, we gave him a little more rope. But he still seemed to have difficulty in obtaining information of real value – or perhaps his aim all along was to come to England.

Be that as it may, he finally booked a passage.

His passport was in order, and our consulate gave him a visa.

When he reached this side he successfully passed the examination officers. He got into the train and proceeded to London. And, all this time, the NID had been kept apprised of his movements.

Half an hour before the boat train was due, the intelligence officer referred to above put on his overcoat and his uniform cap (he was a 'brass hat', and a very senior one at that) and went down to the station. He had made the necessary arrangements with the station authorities. In order to leave the station, all passengers by the boat train had to pass through a room where this officer was standing, and were required either to show their passports or declare their nationality to be British.

It was a purely cursory examination – until our friend the 'neutral' came in. Whether the British intelligence officer acted on the spur of the moment, or whether he had made his plan beforehand, is not known. He would never say. If he had a plan, the 'neutral' played right into his hands. If he had none, his quickness of wit was wonderful.

The 'neutral' handed in his passport, which was passed to the British officer, who was about to inspect it when the man thrust his hands in his trousers pockets and stood there nonchalantly.

Quick as a rapier thrust, the British officer barked out in pure German:

'How dare you stand like that before a superior officer?'

The 'neutral' automatically brought his heels together with a click, and half-stiffened to attention. Then he suddenly relaxed, and tried to look as if he had not grasped the meaning of the words.

'I was led to believe that you did not understand German, *Herr Hauptmann*,' said the British intelligence officer, quietly slipping the passport into his overcoat pocket. 'There is a car outside. Will you be good enough to come with me?'

The German captain went. The game was up.

Sharp eyesight and quick wits on the part of a boarding officer detailed to look out for German agents travelling from America to the Continent did us good service on another occasion.

A certain Herr Boehm had got through to America by way of Holland in the autumn of 1914, and there became a very active member of Count Bernstorff's group of secret service agents. We kept track of him fairly well in the United States, but he seemed to be a more or less useless person, who talked a great deal and apparently did very little. He considered himself to be occupied solely with the Higher Political Aspects (nothing but capitals will do justice to the importance of those words), and took no part in the terrorist campaign.

Then, suddenly, we lost sight of him.

It was quite possible he was up to mischief somewhere in the United States. Or he might be on his way home. Anyway, the ports were warned.

One day a neutral steamer came into harbour to drop passengers for Britain. Passports were, of course, examined, whether the passengers were landing here or not.

Among those going on to a continental port was a certain Mr Thrasher. His accent was pure American. His clothes were American. His passport was American. He corresponded to the description on it, even down to the spectacles.

The boarding officers cross-examined him in the usual way, but were unable to shake his story. One of them, however, noticed that Mr Thrasher's spectacles seemed to bother him. It looked as if he were not used to wearing spectacles.

Quite conversationally and sympathetically, the boarding officer asked him about his eyesight – who was his oculist, what was the disability with his eyes, and so on.

Mr Thrasher became confused. His replies were muddled and contradictory. He didn't seem to know much about his own eyesight. So he was politely but firmly taken ashore for more cross-examination, and ultimately admitted that he was the missing Herr Boehm. He spent the rest of the war in a British internment camp, because, after all, he had done no spying in this country, and we had no evidence that he had ever sent any information to Germany.

There was an amusing sequel to the capture of Herr Boehm. A few months later some papers of Count Bernstorff fell into our hands, among them a report from the German Military Information Bureau dated March 1916. It dealt with the activities of Herr Boehm, and suggested, not too delicately, that he was too free with his tongue for the good of his service! He was recommended for recall.

That, then, was why he had left America so secretly.

CHAPTER 16

FIGHTING THE WRECKERS
IN AMERICA

T HE LATE PRESIDENT Wilson, in his address to Congress in 1915, devoted all the opening passages to a denunciation of certain 'citizens of the United States, I blush to think, born under other flags', who had devoted themselves wholeheartedly to the cause of Germany by running a guerrilla war of their own in the United States.

'They have formed plots to destroy property,' the President said. 'They have entered into conspiracies against the neutrality of the government. They have sought to pry into every confidential transaction of the government.'

The indictment was fully deserved. The lawlessness of the modern gunmen is almost mild compared with the reign of terror initiated by the anti-Ally gangs in the United States as soon as the war began.

In the early months, as the American authorities themselves subsequently admitted, the methods of dealing with this outbreak of organised outrage were lax. At that time it fell to the lot of the British ID to take a hand in the work in defence of British interests. It was a difficult and delicate task, of course, but it was done so diplomatically, and the evidence gathered and placed before the American authorities was so strong, that before long four or five departments, including the police, were actively on the trail. It was no uncommon thing for a suspect who had been denounced by the British ID agents to be shadowed by men from four US departments at once!

This was publicity with a vengeance – and even where no case could be made out for an arrest, the 'silent pressure' of the watching was generally enough to drive the delinquent into retirement.

The names of Captain von Papen and Captain Boy-Ed, of Paul Koenig, Dr Albert, and Dr Dernburg are notorious throughout the world. It is perhaps worth pointing out, as a testimony to the discretion with which the British intelligence system was worked in the United States, that not a single name of any of our men has ever been mentioned in any paper, either with bouquets or with abuse. And yet American papers in 1915 stated that there were then more than 200 British secret service agents at work all over the states, countering the machinations of von Papen's satellites.

They had all sorts of different crimes to keep under observation. There was the forging of passports, which if it had not been watched very carefully would have given us endless trouble in Europe. That this forging was personally supervised by Boy-Ed so long as he was in the United States formed part of the indictment by the Federal Grand Jury in 1916, and the faking was very ingeniously done. Fortunately we had a man working in the 'passport factory' – as we had at the heart of most of the other German activities – and were therefore able to trace most of the fakes that were in circulation.

Thus we came into possession of a list of German reservist officers living in America who were to be shipped to the fatherland by whatever means offered, and for whom forged passports were to be provided by the factory.

The attempts to bribe labour leaders and to foment strikes in the munition works and other establishments making war material for the Allies were almost ceaseless for the first year of the war. These were so much a domestic affair of the American government's, however, that beyond gathering all the information we could and passing it to the proper authorities, we took only a small part in dealing with that branch of the German campaign.

The maintenance of a watch on the interned German ships was our most difficult task. It is a great testimony to the work of those who were engaged in this task that so few German ships got away at all. There was the case of the *Sacramento*, which escaped from San Francisco in the autumn of 1914 and served as a supply ship to von Spee's Squadron until she was sunk after the Battle of the Falklands. But even in this case we had our revenge, for all the necessary evidence was collected to bring about the indictment of those who plotted the escape.

In another case we brought together the evidence necessary to indict the American managing director of the Hamburg–Amerika line, with his purchasing agent and a superintendent, for conspiring to supply false clearance papers to vessels that were to slip out with supplies for the German warships still at large during 1914. This was one of the schemes of Captain Boy-Ed, run from his secret office at No. 11, Broadway, New York.

Several stores of arms were collected in various parts of the United States to German order. Some of these, there is no doubt, were intended for despatch to the German Army, but as that became less and less possible, the German plotters turned their attention to exporting them to disaffected people in the British Empire. Thus there was a store in West Houston Street, New York, with arms and munitions enough for 10,000 men. One item was 2,500,000 rounds of rifle cartridges. These were to have been shipped in the autumn of 1915, and plans were most carefully laid for the secret embarkation of the whole consignment.

Our ID men knew all about it. They had had their eyes on that store for quite a long time – in fact, ever since it came into existence in the early summer. And quite suddenly, a day or two before the Germans had arranged to send the stuff afloat, there was a marked concentration of British cruisers off New York. It was so noticeable that all the American papers commented on it, and wondered what on earth it was all about.

The Germans knew, and those munitions were never shipped. They were seized by the United States authorities about four months later.

It will be remembered that in one of Count Bernstorff's letters, found among the von Papen papers seized at Falmouth and deciphered in the famous Room 40 at the admiralty, there was a reference to 'arms stored to our account in New York and the state of Washington, which were intended for India.'

The fomenting of rebellion in India, Ireland, and other parts of the empire was carried on very vigorously by the officials of the German embassy in Washington. They spent a lot of money on it, all to no purpose, and we were on their trail pretty well all the time. Their association with Sir Roger Casement and the

Easter Rebellion in Dublin is now a matter of history, and need not be retold here.

One of the things that, when it became known, caused the most bitter feeling against the plotters among genuine Americans, was the extent to which German officials were involved in the dastardly plot for firing liners at sea by means of incendiary bombs. In 1917 the United States government Public Information Committee issued a pamphlet with photographic copies of documents inculpating Captain Koenig and Captain von Papen in the plot. But it was the British secret service that collected the evidence on which the Americans were able to act.

Altogether some forty-one cases of fire breaking out in ships that had left New York were listed by the Federal Grand Jury in the ultimate indictment of the villains of the piece.

Two men actively connected with that foul business were Kleist and Scheele. Their names are probably forgotten by the world at large by now, but at the time of the trial they were headlines in the news.

The inner story of the detection of the bomb factory and its ramifications did not come out at the trial, but it is worth putting on record.

One day the head of the British intelligence service in New York was rung up on the telephone and heard a voice, of distinctly Teutonic accent, speaking in a very nervous tone.

Did Captain ------ want some information of great importance to Britain? said the Voice. If so, would he send someone who spoke German to an address in Hoboken?

The voice was invited to come to New York, but flatly declined. Hoboken or nowhere was his ultimatum.

One of our men who spoke German like a native was sent

to the rendezvous, but was warned to be on his guard, for the whole thing reeked of a trap. Count Bernstorff's minions were very active at that time.

Down in Hoboken, near the Hamburg–Amerika piers, our man found the address he had been given, a small German café. At the door he was met by an obvious German-American who seemed to expect him, and directed him upstairs to the first floor. The ID man had his hand on his gun all the time. The position looked more and more dangerous.

And it was no better when he met his informant – a weedy, terrified youth, who might really have been the tethered goat in a trap for a tiger. This youth gave his name, the same as that mentioned on the telephone, and suggested that they should go into a private room.

The ID man was not falling into that trap. He suggested a corner in the public refreshment room. There was less scope for an 'unfortunate incident' there – and, anyway, it was he who sat with his back to the wall.

The informant told part of his tale. A clever German chemist had enlisted a gang of men to make and place incendiary bombs in Allied merchant ships sailing from American ports. And for the names of the plotters the youth asked $2,000 (£400).

The ID man was not such a fool as to carry that amount of money on him in Hoboken, and he wanted more evidence before he paid. He produced a $20 bill as evidence of good faith, and promised more if the youth would bring him one of the bombs next day.

He did so. It was a leaden case, 4 inches long by 1 inch in diameter, with a smaller cylinder of zinc inside it. A corrosive acid was contained in this, which would ignite the other ingredients in the lead container when it had eaten its way through the inner cylinder. The time it took to do that depended on the thickness of the zinc.

The youth would part with no more information without his price. So he got it – but by that time the Bomb Squad of the New York Police, under the famous Inspector Tunney, was in the game. The youth was arrested with the dollars on him, and asked to account for them.

Mr Tunney had a way of asking questions that somehow compelled answers. So the youth came out with the whole story. The chemist was a Dr Walter Scheele, his chief assistant was Kleist, and the bomb factory was actually on board the interned German liner *Friedrich der Grosse*.

Most important of all, the trail led to more information incriminating Wolf von Igel, the pseudo 'advertising agent' of Wall Street, and one of the leaders of the German terrorist organisation.

All our countering of German activities in the United States, of course, had to be done by guile. We could not use force, and, in the early months at any rate, we could not call in the law. But guile served us very well, as Dr Albert has good reason to know.

The great financial expert of the German embassy, who was also paymaster of the gangsters, had a number of documents that he wanted to send to Berlin. There was an obstacle in the way. He suspected, not unreasonably, that the British government might be interested in those documents, and, as the British Navy maintained a very strict watch on seaborne traffic, the Herr Doctor was compelled to use stratagem to get his papers through the blockade.

He made arrangements for them to be shipped by a Swedish

liner, in the name of a Swedish firm, and to be forwarded to Berlin from Stockholm.

He laid his plans in the greatest secrecy and with the utmost care. Only three people in his office knew about the papers – himself, Captain von Papen, and his typist.

This young woman, avowedly a keen pro-German American, was very diligent. She was so energetic that the day before the case containing the papers was to be sent away she would not even leave the office to have her lunch. She had some food brought in to her, and she squatted actually on the precious box itself while she ate her meal.

Captain von Papen was no less diligent. Neither he nor Dr Albert would allow that case out of the sight of one or other of them. And so, while the typist lunched, Captain von Papen was in the room, too.

It must not be supposed that he was 'vamped.' Indeed, there was no need for feminine wiles. The Captain fancied himself as a ladies' man, and he proposed to keep in practice by a little flirtation with the typist.

Soon they were sitting side by side on the precious case, and the lady was coy. Absent-mindedly she took a red lead pencil, and, quite without thinking, drew two large red hearts side by side on the woodwork of the case.

Pretty conceit! The gallant Captain took the pencil from her and himself drew the arrow to transfix the two hearts.

Arcadian simplicity!

All that the searchers had to do when the steamer called at the British port for examination was to look for a wooden case marked in red with two large hearts joined by an arrow.

They found it.

But Dr Albert never knew that his own right-hand man had betrayed him, however unintentionally, and had placed at the disposal of the American government priceless documentary evidence to build up the case that led ultimately to the expulsion from America of von Papen and Boy-Ed.

All through his activities in the United States von Papen blundered egregiously. That list from Albert's office, containing a long report on German spy efforts in America and a list of payments to various agents all over the country, was only one of the innumerable examples of how he played right into the hands of the British counter-espionage.

Another of his blunders, or at any rate a blunder in his office, enabled us to decipher one of the most awkward codes that the German secret service used.

It was a four-fold code. If one part of the communication fell into the wrong hands, it was indecipherable without the other three parts.

There were four letters involved in the system. Each letter contained certain words, and each was sent to a different address.

Thus, the first sentence of Letter Number One contained the first, fifth, ninth, and thirteenth words, and thereafter every fourth word of the complete document. Letter Number Two contained the second, sixth, tenth, and fourteenth words, and so on.

An example will make the code clear:

Letter Number One began, let us say, 'You letter other are'

Letter Number Two began, 'Know is directions coming'

Letter Number Three began, 'Whence coming other I'

Letter Number Four began, 'This from letters ask'

If those words are set out exactly over one another we get the sense:

You	*letter*	*other*	*are*
know	*is*	*directions*	*coming,*
whence	*coming,*	*other*	*I*
this	*from*	*letters*	*ask.*

Read each column downwards and the words fall into place. Punctuation has been put in to facilitate the reading.

Von Papen's office received several letters in that code, addressed originally, of course, to various people in New York who were part of the gang, and the complete groups were kept pinned together in the files. A smart clerk in the office, who by some chance had a lot of friends in the British intelligence service, got them together one day and made some quite interesting discoveries.

Without claiming too great credit for their cleverness, it is reasonable to say that the British intelligence men in the United States were always masters of their German opponents, and, so far as wiliness was concerned, had them 'beaten to a frazzle'. And this applies not only to men in the higher ranks of the business. There is the singular case of the marine servant. Only Kipling could tell it as it should be told. Here we cannot do more than outline the story as we heard it, after the war, in the gloaming of a Scapa evening, while with the Squadron that was still guarding the then unsunken German fleet.

It is the story of how Captain Paul Koenig was doubly hoodwinked by one of our men in New York.

The British ID man had a modest apartment in one of the less prosperous quarters of New York. He was not officially in America at all, but he had with him his marine servant, who passed for a valet, secretary, chauffeur and companion. This marine was a man slow of speech and heavy of appearance, but with an agile brain behind his bucolic exterior.

Below the ID man's apartment lived a young German, and what had taken our agent into that neighbourhood was the fact that this young German was suspected of being an active member (how active was just what we wanted to know) of the German terrorist gangs.

This young man struck up an acquaintance with the marine. In a slow-witted way the valet let it appear that his master was 'up to something.' He also let it appear that he had himself a streak of greediness in him. Money was a grand thing to have, honestly if possible, but still…

The young German felt his way cautiously. He, on his part, suffered from curiosity. He would like to know, quite innocently, of course, what was the truth about the supply of munitions from American factories to Britain, and what arrangements the British had for protecting them at sea. But most of all he thought it would be thrilling to know who really were the men who were doing secret service work for Britain in the United States.

And, when the seed had been planted, he watered it with a suggestion of payment.

The marine undertook to try to find out from friends of his in New York, but he cannily insisted that he must first see the real head of the German secret service in order to satisfy himself about payment. And the Germans fell into the trap!

The man was conducted by his young friend, after dark, to the office of the Hamburg–Amerika Line in lower Broadway. There was an elaborate ritual of passwords, locked doors, long passages, and revolvers on desks – all the trappings of the Spy

King of melodrama, in fact. And ultimately the marine found himself being presented to – Captain Paul Koenig.

Score No. 1 for our ID! The head of the branch, if not the head of the whole organisation, was found.

Herr Koenig was very anxious to find out who were his opponents. How did the British ID get its reports? Could the marine give him a complete list of those who worked for the British secret service ?

The marine chewed slowly on the idea, pondering it, and eventually said he thought he might have a try.

He did – with the help of his master.

There were a number of young 'gun-shy' men of British origin in the United States, who always looked mysterious when they were asked what they were doing for their country, and sometimes went so far as to whisper very confidentially: 'secret service!'

Marine and master got them on the list.

They also had names of the employees of the German and Austrian consulates. Several of these were dropped haphazard into the list for Captain Koenig.

The marine was conducted to Captain Koenig's 'citadel' again. And the list was duly paid for!

Score No. 2 for the British ID. Some of the British 'Cuthberts' had a most exciting life for the next few weeks, shadowed everywhere by German secret service agents! And as for the German and Austrian consular employees, life became an absolute burden to them until it dawned on Captain Koenig that he had been sold.

The comedy of Dr Albert's attaché case is fairly well known, though it is not always remembered that it was the papers found therein that definitely linked the Germans with the Casement case and the Easter Rebellion.

Credit for the feat has been claimed for a reporter on the *Providence Journal* (Rhode Island), a paper that certainly ran a most effective counter-espionage campaign of its own for months before the American authorities really tackled the business. But it has also been ascribed to a man who was working for the British ID. Whoever the hero may have been, it was a neatly planned piece of work.

The watcher trailed Dr Albert to a leather goods shop, and there found him buying a new attaché case. The bright idea struck him to have one like it, and also to get to know exactly what the initials on it looked like after they had been executed to the Doctor's order. So the purchase was left at the shop till the next day, until the customer could be shown the finished case for Dr Albert.

When he saw it, he decided that initials would not improve the appearance of his own case, so he took it away – to another shop, where he had Dr Albert's initials put on in the exact style of that gentleman's case.

A day or two later, complete with attaché case, he followed Dr Albert (also complete with case) into one of the trains on the elevated railway. He started a scuffle in the crowded carriage, and, in the confusion, changed the two cases. Dr Albert went away with an empty one, and at the next station the watcher got out – with a full case.

The real humour of the situation is that Dr Albert did not appear to realise that he had been tricked, and actually went to the police for help in recovering his missing property.

But they did not find it.

As the months went by the British ID gathered and passed to the American authorities a mass of evidence about the activities of the terrorists – how they tried to foment dock strikes to prevent ships sailing, to introduce explosives into munition works, to damage the Welland Canal, the Soo Canal and the Lehigh Valley railway. There were attempts to damage the cables to Europe, particularly those of the Western Union, and a great deal of thieving went on that was not the work of the regular criminal classes. Motor cars and lorries awaiting shipment on the dockside were damaged, and tyres stolen, and men who were caught in the act were described by the police as being above the average intelligence and not ordinary thieves.

One really curious little incident arose quite by accident. One of our men was asked by an acquaintance (who had no idea of his real mission in the states) if he had ever seen a travelling trunk with secret drawers.

Our agent pretended not to be particularly interested, but said that, out of idle curiosity, he wouldn't mind looking at such a thing if it existed. But when the acquaintance tried to arrange for him to see a specimen, difficulties arose.

After a time, however, and by dint of very careful inquiry, our man found out the factory where these interesting oddities were made. And careful watch was kept on the place to discover the people who were buying them. Two such trunks were traced to a certain gentleman, who was found to have booked a passage to Bergen.

Then he did a curious thing. He sailed without the trunks!

Still we watched, and the trunks went down to the docks to be shipped by the next steamer of the same line.

So we thought it was time the American customs took a hand in the game, and they were advised about the trunks that were to travel alone. Two men came down to the pier and set about embarking the luggage, whereupon customs stepped in and seized the trunks. They were emptied and examined, and the secret compartments were found to be full of confidential papers, with, in addition, a consignment of dental rubber!

The papers proved to be unconnected with German secret service work, but the rubber was an interesting find, as it indicated another way in which small consignments of badly needed commodities were slipping through the British blockade and examination service.

CHAPTER 17

GAMBLING ON 'THE DAY'

N O READER OF the foregoing pages will be disposed to underrate the contribution of the naval intelligence department to the Allied victory at sea. It was, indeed, not the least potent of the factors that, collectively, immobilised the German Navy – apart from its U-boats – and, in the end, brought about its demoralisation and defeat.

We have seen how our intelligence system, operating before the war, safeguarded us from naval surprises that, had they been sprung without warning, might have led to reverses far more serious than those we did sustain. We have seen, too, how the same system, expanded and developed to cope with the manifold and complex problems of war itself, functioned with an efficiency that to those unversed in the secrets of its mechanism seemed to border on the supernatural.

To intelligence work we owed in great measure the success of our anti-submarine campaign, as also the maintenance of that unsleeping watch on the High Seas Fleet that enabled us to forestall every move it made. Again, without the cooperation of the NID the blockade of the central powers, which steadily sapped their stamina and endurance, would have remained incomplete and largely ineffective.

It now remains to tell of the part played by intelligence work in circumventing the German Navy's last and most ambitious scheme of operations, the collapse of which hastened the Revolution and swept the Teutonic war lords from the stage where they had strutted over-long.

The story of this crowning achievement properly begins in May 1918. Towards the close of that month the German High Command could no longer conceal from the nation, still less from itself, the failure of the great submarine gamble on which it had embarked early in 1917. Millions of tonnes of shipping had been destroyed, it is true, and the U-boats were still exacting a regular toll in the Channel, the Atlantic and the Mediterranean.

But, contrary to the most positive prediction, the Allies had not been reduced to starvation within six months. After fifteen months of ruthless submarine warfare their vital communications remained still intact, they were fighting with unimpaired vigour, and they had been joined by a new and mighty associate whose resources in manpower and material were well-nigh illimitable. Since the entry of the United States was directly due to the U-boat campaign, this weapon might even be said to have recoiled on the heads of those who wielded it. At all events, even the optimists at German GHQ now realised that victory was not to be won by submarines alone.

Nor did the military situation afford consolation for this grave disappointment. The great offensive launched in March had not achieved the results promised by Ludendorff: the Allied front, though sorely battered and deeply indented, still held firm. Thanks to the influx of American troops, pouring across the Atlantic in unchecked and ever-swelling volume, the manpower of the Allies was rapidly increasing, while that of Germany was steadily wasting away. Ludendorff, it is true, was planning further offensives, but hopes of accomplishing a complete and decisive breakthrough were growing dim. In short, from the German point of view the war position as a whole was already becoming desperate. It was at this critical juncture that the idea of throwing in the High Seas Fleet to redress the balance occurred to the minds of the German war leaders.

Admiral Scheer had urged this plan repeatedly, but hitherto without success. The Kaiser was still disinclined to risk his precious battleships, while a strong political element continued to advocate the preservation of the fleet as a bargaining asset at the Peace Conference. But in view of the gravity of the outlook, this opposition was weakening. In May, therefore, the Kaiser gave his conditional sanction to the initial preparations for a great naval offensive. As we shall see, however, the naval command eventually decided to flout the Kaiser by ignoring the conditions he had laid down.

At German GHQ it seems to have been accepted as a matter of course that the High Seas Fleet was in perfect fighting fettle. But the British Admiralty had reason to think otherwise. Nearly a year previously our intelligence agents in Germany had begun to report signs of demoralisation among the German naval personnel. In the summer of 1917 these reports were corroborated by actual, if isolated, cases of mutiny at Kiel and Wilhelmshaven. They were suppressed with an iron hand, but from the information that continued to come through from our ID men, it was clear that the mischief was only scotched, not eradicated.

Several causes combined to sap the fighting spirit of the German lower deck. In the first place, the obvious reluctance of the high command to seek another pitched battle with the British fleet was not lost on the men, who naturally and rightly concluded that their leaders felt no confidence in the outcome of such an action. Still officially claimed as a 'victory' for propaganda purposes, the Battle of Jutland was now recognised by all ranks and ratings in the High Seas Fleet as an indecisive encounter in which the German forces had narrowly escaped disaster. During the brief period they were in contact with the British main fleet they suffered a merciless hammering that gave them a new respect for the terrible broadsides of the Grand Fleet. 'Never again,' was the general verdict, according to Captain Persius – qualified, in the case of the High Command, by a resolve to accept battle again only under the most favourable circumstances, and with the mass cooperation of submarines and airships.

This plan was actually tried in August 1916, though with indifferent success. On that occasion, so hastily did Admiral Scheer scurry back to his base, on receiving what proved to be an erroneous Zeppelin report of the advance of the main British fleet, that the humblest member of the lower-deck cannot have failed to draw the obvious conclusion. Thus, we may assume, were implanted the first seeds of defeatism which were destined in the course of two years to grow into a upas tree.

Another factor undoubtedly responsible in great measure for the weakening of morale was the British minelaying activity in the Bight. After two years of war we had at length evolved a thoroughly effective type of mine, and when intensive manufacture had given us the necessary material, we began a systematic and widespread operation for the purpose of mining every channel used by the High Seas Fleet and its auxiliary forces. Vessels of all types, from battleships to submarines and converted liners, were employed in this work. How many mines in all were laid is not known, but the twentieth destroyer flotilla alone – 'one of the corps d'élite of the navy', as it was aptly designated by Sir Eric Geddes – dropped over 22,000.

Although they suffered losses from this cause in 1917, it was not until the spring of 1918 that the Germans began to experience the full effects of our vigorous mining policy. Then casualties came thick and fast. Minesweeping flotillas were shattered; patrol craft detailed to escort outgoing and returning submarines were blown up wholesale, while many of their charges met a like fate. During the first six months of 1918 more than a hundred German vessels were destroyed in and about the Bight – that is, at the rate of four a week. No squadron or flotilla could move from its anchorage without the almost certain risk of losing units.

A vivid picture of what the Germans suffered at this period was drawn by the late Admiral Scheer in his war diary, from which the following notes are extracted:

> The number of mines laid in the North Sea during 1917–18 grew steadily greater. Almost daily we suffered losses among the minesweeping craft, while among the ships used to escort the U-boats in their passage through the minefields there had been so many losses that in March 1917 the fleet had only four such vessels left. On 29 March the outpost boat Bismarck ran on a mine and sank; only three of the crew could be saved.
>
> 11 May – Minesweeping according to plan. New mines are observed, and the leading boat of the 5th half-flotilla strikes one and sinks.

Four men missing, including the commanding officer of the half-flotilla.

14 May – Orion, *one of the third minesweeping flotilla, reports that submarine* U-59, *which was being convoyed out to sea, and the minesweeper* Fulda, *have struck mines and sunk.*

15 May – *While trying to get into communication with* U-59 *by tapping, the outpost boat* Heinrich Rathjen *strikes a mine and sinks.*

16 May – *The auxiliary minesweeping flotilla is to mark the spot of* U-59's *accident and try to get into communication with the submarine by tapping. In the course of these operations minesweeper No. 14 hits a mine, and in attempting to reach her the torpedo boat No. 78 does likewise. Both boats sink. Attempts to communicate with* U-59 *must consequently be given up.*

The same night torpedo boat S-27, of the outpost flotilla, hits a mine and sinks while convoying U-86. *And so it went on from day to day.*

There is ample evidence to prove that these unceasing losses from British mines shook the nerves of the German personnel. The supply of volunteers for the minesweeping service (*Himmelfahrts-Dienst*, or 'ascension service', as the German sailors named it in grim jest) soon failed, and men had to be drafted to the vessels. After the war an officer of the German Navy made the following significant admission:

Next to the blockade, the intensive British minelaying was the chief cause of our collapse at sea. For the first two years of the war we laughed at your mines, which often failed to explode, and, when they did explode, only shook us up a bit. But after that we ceased to laugh. Mines began to sprout by the thousand, and every time one exploded it blew a ship to pieces. From 1917 onward our Bight minesweeping formations were known as the 'Suicide Club.'

We lost ships almost daily, sometimes two or three a day. It often happened that one of our swept channels, reported absolutely safe and clear at dusk, would be found at dawn heavily mined, the first intimation being the blowing-up of some unlucky destroyer or sweeper, or perhaps two or three simultaneously.

A third, and perhaps the most direct, cause of German naval disintegration was the inconsiderate treatment of the bluejackets by their officers. Since the war an intense propaganda campaign has been conducted in Germany by naval officers of the old regime. This movement, which is more or less openly supported by the naval section of the Ministry of Defence, has two objects: the revival of national enthusiasm for a strong fleet, and the restoration of the prestige of the naval officers' corps. Thanks to this mass indoctrination, it is almost universally believed in Germany today that the great fleet mutiny of 1918 was the outcome, not of enemy pressure, but of treason on the part of the 'politicians'. In other words, the 'stab-in-the-back' legend is coming to be accepted as historical truth.

But our intelligence reports from the beginning of 1917 told a different story. Pieced together, they would form a chronological and remarkably accurate record of the growth of the movement in the High Seas Fleet, which culminated in open mutiny. For obvious reasons these cannot be quoted here, but the tale they told has since been repeated in more detail by a German authority, Herr Emil Alboldt, who served for more than twenty years in the Imperial Navy, latterly as warrant officer. His revelations will be new to the British public.

His profound knowledge of conditions in the fleet, before and during the war, made him one of the principal witnesses heard before the Reichstag Committee, which, in 1925, inquired into the causes of the naval débâcle. Writing in no sense as an anti-nationalist, but rather as a passionate lover of his old service, he has drawn up a scathing indictment of those whom he holds responsible for its humiliating end.

According to his account, which is well documented throughout, the German naval personnel began the war in a spirit of confidence, though tempered with a wholesome respect for the British Navy. But as month after month went by without disturbing the somnolence of the High Seas Fleet, which lay idle in its barricaded ports, the fighting spirit of the men gradually waned. Two severe defeats (Heligoland Bight and the Dogger Bank), sustained by German cruiser squadrons through lack of battle-fleet support, caused the sailors to question the capacity of their leaders.

Even the partial success gained at Jutland against the British battlecruisers failed to reassure the men, offset as it was by the heavy punishment inflicted on the battleships by the Grand Fleet's gunfire. Herr Alboldt roundly declares that, but for the misty weather prevailing at Jutland, 'nothing could have prevented the British from shooting our whole fleet to pieces, ship by ship, thanks to their superiority in gun range and speed'. Professional ignorance on the part of the senior officers of the old navy was responsible, he asserts, for the inferior armament and speed of its ships.

But his most sensational disclosures relate to the behaviour of German naval officers in the war – a point constantly emphasised in our intelligence reports of the period. To this factor, more than any other, he attributes the ultimate catastrophe. He paints a vivid picture of the hardships and abuses suffered by the lower-deck personnel. At a time when the men's rations had been reduced to the lowest point, and when such food as was served out was often unfit for human consumption, the officers, he asserts, continued to live on the fat of the land. The usual wine allowance to sick and wounded seamen in hospital had long since been cut off, yet officers' wine parties were of almost daily occurrence.

Sometimes the spectacle of their officers feasting and drinking choice vintages proved too much for the half-starved bluejackets, and ominous incidents occurred. For example, in July 1917 the officers of the battleship *Thüringen* were at luncheon when suddenly a torrent of water from a hosepipe on deck poured down through the wardroom skylight, drenching them all to the skin. 'The culprit was never discovered.' In the same month the officers of the fleet were, at their own request, supplied with automatic pistols for personal protection – a fact, it is interesting to note, mentioned in an ID report at the time.

Discontent on the lower deck was fostered by an extreme severity of discipline, which often assumed the pettiest forms; by high-handed, and even brutal, behaviour on the part of the officers, and by the arbitrary curtailment of leave. In the summer of 1917 – only a year after the 'victory' of Jutland – serious mutinies broke out in several vessels, including the fleet flagship, *Friedrich der Grosse*. On one occasion, at the ceremony of hoisting the colours in this ship, a scrubbing brush was hoisted on the flagstaff in place of the naval ensign, rigging and boat tackle were cut through, and the mutineers threatened to throw the gun sights overboard.

Innumerable instances of arrogant and selfish conduct on the part of officers are cited, based for the most part on official evidence. Herr Alboldt draws a striking contrast between this state of affairs and conditions in the British Navy. From the beginning of the war, he states, the British officers practised self-denial, and so retained the respect and affection of their men.

While the half-starved German sailors were rarely granted leave, were confined to their ships or barracks under iron discipline, and given no opportunities for recreation, the British bluejackets received abundant rations, which differed neither in quantity nor quality from those of the officers; they were encouraged to indulge in all forms of sport, and were treated generally by their superiors as honoured comrades, not as despised underlings. Consequently, the morale and discipline of the British personnel remained at the highest level all through the war.

Of special interest are Herr Alboldt's comments on the proposed sortie of the High Seas Fleet just before the Armistice. Many of the officers, it appears, had been boasting that rather than see the fleet surrendered to the British they would blow it up, or at least cause it to be sunk in battle. The German seamen, however, were in no mind to be led to the slaughter merely to save the prestige of officers whom they despised. They seem to have discussed among themselves the chances that the fleet would have in a pitched battle with the Grand Fleet, and to have come unanimously to the conclusion that crushing defeat was inevitable.

Herr Alboldt gives a long list of cogent reasons for this lack of confidence. In 1918, he states, the British had adopted a highly efficient type of armour-piercing shell, which would have wrought havoc in the strongest German ships, and in view of the

British superiority in range, the Germans could not have hoped to escape. Moreover, the new and 'secret' minefields on which the German fleet was to rely for the protection of its flanks had already been discovered by the British. (That is perfectly true. Thanks in part to the close watch kept on German minelayers by our patrol craft, particularly submarines, and in part to our intelligence reports from the enemy bases, the position of every new minefield became known to us almost immediately after it had been laid.)

Reverting to the 'stab-in-the-back' legend now being circulated by former naval officers, Herr Alboldt declares that if such an assassin's blow were really struck, it can only have come from the navy itself. In this connection he cites Professor Birk, one of the leading citizens of Kiel, who has written:

> *I have a feeling of unexampled indignation at the conduct of the navy, which in the fatherland's supreme hour of need stabbed the army in the back, and thus brought about the peace terms under which we now live. Never in the world has there been a greater act of treason than that committed by the German Navy in November 1918. The magnitude of this crime and its terrible consequences have wiped out from the memory of the German people all former services rendered by the navy.*

It should be added that Herr Alboldt's credentials as a well-informed and conscientious witness are vouched for by Professor Walther Schücking, who was chairman of the Reichstag Committee that investigated the antecedents of the German collapse, and who has written an introduction to Alboldt's remarkable book.

Apart from our intelligence reports from Germany, the first

intimation we had that the German naval command was planning some important move came in a curiously negative fashion. In the spring of 1918 we found that German minelaying operations in the Dover Patrol area, and also in the Channel, were becoming much less extensive; in fact, they all but ceased in the Dover Patrol zone. Most of this work had been done by the small *UC* submarine minelayers based on Bruges. Originally there had been seventy-nine of these venomous little craft, and, as our intelligence records showed, nearly forty of them were still in existence at the beginning of 1918. Yet, as time went on, it became more and more difficult to discover their whereabouts. Beyond the fact that they had obviously left Bruges we had no information about them – for a time.

But the mystery was very soon cleared up by the ID. It was found that all the *UC* boats had been sent back to Wilhelmshaven and Cuxhaven, whence they were making periodical trips across the North Sea, loaded to capacity with mines. What, then, was their mission? It was nothing less than the sowing of a great belt of mines off the Firth of Tay, some 45 miles east of the Bell Rock. As soon as a *UC* boat had dropped its deadly cargo in the appointed place, closing up another gap in the ever-extending arc, it returned to one or other of the German North Sea bases for a fresh load. Throughout the summer they came and went with timetable regularity, the minefield steadily grew in length and width, and the German naval command firmly believed the whole operation to be going on in profound secrecy.

They were wrong. As early as June 1918 we knew all about it. Once the *UC* flotilla had been re-located, it was comparatively easy to keep its units under observation, and the fact that they were building up a gigantic mine barrier in a certain area left no doubt as to the purpose in view. This was to ambush the

Grand Fleet as it sailed out of its bases. Clearly, then, a dash to the south by the British battle fleet in full force was anticipated by the Germans, and what else than a grand sortie by the High Seas Fleet could occasion such a move? We knew, then, on the strongest circumstantial evidence, that the enemy was meditating a great naval offensive, and, armed with this knowledge, it was a simple matter to take the requisite precautions.

We had no difficulty in locating the 'secret' mine barrage. Large sections of it were removed by our minesweepers, but certain patches – after being meticulously noted on our confidential charts – were left in place, to serve as an added protection to the approaches to our own fleet bases and, perhaps, as a menace to enemy raiders or U-boats. To the very end of the war the Germans remained ignorant of the discovery of their 'secret', and assumed the immense minefield laid by their *UC* boats to be unsuspected and intact.

As the summer wore on, evidence of the impending sortie accumulated in ever-increasing volume, mostly supplied by our intelligence agents. Battleships, battlecruisers, and light cruisers of the High Seas Fleet were going into dockyard in rotation, where they were overhauled and furbished up in readiness for action. Gunnery and torpedo practice was held almost continuously, for the most part in the Baltic, where there was less danger of interruption from British submarines. Shipwrights and artificers were released from the army to swell the dockyard staffs at Kiel and Wilhelmshaven, both to hasten the preparation of the fleet and to be in readiness to execute repairs on such ships as returned to port after the great battle in the North Sea. A grim but conclusive piece of evidence was supplied by the enlargement of hospital accommodation at the principal bases.

Incredible as it may seem, the British Admiralty knew far more about the proposed sortie than did the German Navy itself. This was due to the strict secrecy in which the plan was shrouded by the German naval command, which realised that even a whisper of what was toward would jeopardise the whole scheme. Admiral von Trotha, the then chief of staff, has since explained why the elaborate precautions to prevent any leakage were necessary. In his evidence before the Reichstag Committee of inquiry into the German collapse, held in 1925–26, he said that owing to the comparative proximity of the Dutch frontier and the crowds of people who came into Wilhelmshaven every day from the surrounding country, there was an ever-present danger that news of any unusual movement by the fleet would be known across the border in a few hours. (He might have added, with truth, that such news did almost invariably leak through to Holland, and thence to London, while it was still fresh.)

Consequently, on this occasion, the naval staff endeavoured to confine the secret to the narrowest circle possible. Of the twenty officers comprising the staff itself, only one-third were made acquainted with the plans. No documents relating to the scheme were sent to imperial GHQ at Spa, nor was it proposed to send any until the fleet was actually at sea. Moreover, said Admiral von Trotha, 'we had to use extraordinary care when making wireless signals, because the wireless directional stations of the British had become so skilful that, by reasoning from the coded orders sent out by the German wireless stations, they knew whenever a ship came into the roadstead at Wilhelmshaven'.

Questioned as to why the crews of the High Seas Fleet were given no warning of what was intended, the admiral again took refuge behind the plea of secrecy; but other witnesses admitted that there were grave doubts as to the men's reception of the news: in other words, the discipline and fighting spirit of the personnel were no longer considered to be above reproach.

When the evidence tendered to the Reichstag Committee seven years later is examined closely, there emerges a story that would be quite unbelievable were it not so fully documented. It is, in effect, the story of a conspiracy by the high naval command to torpedo the negotiations for an armistice that were already in train, to defy Kaiser and Cabinet, and to stake the future of the fatherland on a desperate gamble. If the projected naval offensive had proved victorious, the results, however brilliant, could not possibly have turned the tide of war in Germany's favour. Even if the Grand Fleet had lost half its ships, the combined naval resources of the Allies would still have been far greater than those of Germany. Thus, the re-establishment of the blockade would have been only a matter of time, and the flow of American troops across the Atlantic would not have been seriously interrupted. Had Germany won a naval victory in October 1918 she would merely have prolonged her own agony.

But, in fact, the prospect of such a victory was remote, and had the proposed sortie of the High Seas Fleet ended in disaster Germany would have found herself in an infinitely worse position than before. She would have been held to have broken faith with the Allies, to have used the armistice negotiations as a cloak for treachery, and her punishment would have been merciless. When Germans complain of the severity of the Treaty of Versailles they might profitably reflect on the terrible price they would have had to pay if this sinister naval conspiracy had not been frustrated in the nick of time.

CHAPTER 18

FALSE DAWN

BEFORE EXPLAINING IN greater detail the German naval plans for 'The Day' and how they were defeated, it may be as well to emphasise the absolute unanimity of all the evidence available on this subject, whether from the German side or from our intelligence reports of the period. We have to thank the Reichstag Committee of 1925–26 for many illuminating and dramatic revelations, elicited in the course of its exhaustive inquiry into the antecedents of the surrender. While these were new to the world at large, they were fully known to the British Admiralty in 1918. Among the witnesses called upon to testify as to the projected naval offensive of October 1918 were Vice-Admiral von Trotha, Rear-Admiral Heinrich (chief of the torpedo-boat flotillas), Rear-Admiral von Levetzow, General Gröner, General von Kuhl, Professor Hans Delbrück, and Dr Eugen Fischer, Herr Scheidemann, and Herr Otto Wels, the Socialist leaders.

The date of the High Seas Fleet offensive was to be 28 October 1918 – that is, nearly a month after General Ludendorff had demanded an immediate armistice as the only means of saving his armies from utter disaster. Thereupon the German government opened negotiations with President Wilson, and it was while these were proceeding that Admiral Scheer – who had recently relinquished the command of the fleet to become chief of staff – had an audience of the Kaiser at Potsdam, in which he begged for a free hand with the fleet, pointing out that since it was no longer required as a cover for U-boat operations, it ought to be employed in its proper mission of seeking battle with the enemy.

There is no doubt that the Kaiser accepted this view in principle. He did not, however, give his consent to any definite plan, for the sufficient reason that none was submitted to him. Admiral Scheer, conscious of his Imperial Master's reluctance to risk his beloved battleships, deemed it prudent not to reveal the desperate project he had in view. He went on with his preparations without asking for the Kaiser's sanction, because, as he subsequently admitted, he was afraid he might not get it.

Nor was it only the Kaiser who was to be kept in the dark. The then Chancellor, Prince Max of Baden, was not consulted, though he was already deeply involved in the armistice negotiations and had given an undertaking to abandon the U-boat campaign. In his own narrative of events he states that he first heard of the naval plan on 2 November, whereas the decisive battle had been timed for 28 October, and had been cancelled on account of mutiny on 31 October. The first intimation he received of what had been going on behind his back was a request from Admiral Scheer that he should sign a manifesto addressed to the crews of the fleet, assuring them that there was no intention of sending the fleet on a 'death cruise', and appealing for the maintenance of discipline.

This official repudiation of the 'death cruise' plan, which the Chancellor was inveigled into signing, was, no doubt, correct, strictly speaking, since the naval command expected a victory, not a disaster. Nevertheless it was misleading, in that it was read, and intended to be read, as meaning that there was no question of seeking action with the British fleet, but only of a routine practice cruise for training purposes. Clearly, therefore, the admirals were determined to hoodwink both the Cabinet and the men of the fleet, to seek a pitched battle on their own, and, if fortune did not smile on them, to pretend that the expected encounter with the British fleet had been accidental.

They were preparing to embark on this desperate venture without the sanction of the Supreme War Lord, who was also their Commander-in-Chief; in flat defiance of the Cabinet; in full knowledge that Germany's honour was already pledged in the conduct of the peace negotiations then in train, and also in the knowledge that their own men would not obey them if the truth of the cruise leaked out! The annals of history may be searched in vain for a parallel to this crazy and unscrupulous attempt by a few admirals to override all authority and stake the future of their country on a single throw of the dice.

Crazy the adventure unquestionably was. Now that the complete facts are known, enabling the chances to be weighed, it can be said with positive certainty that the odds against success were a hundred to one. This opinion is notoriously held by many, if not a majority, of German experts, several of whom testified in that sense before the Reichstag Committee.

The calculations of the admirals who planned the enterprise

were based on false premises. On their own admission, absolute secrecy was an essential pre-condition of success, yet the secret had long since been discovered by the British. That Admiral Scheer and his colleagues should have believed it possible to keep all their elaborate preparations from the enemy's knowledge – preparations that extended over many months and included the mining of a vast area of open sea – does not say much for their sagacity.

As outlined in the remarkably accurate forecasts by our intelligence department, the plan involved the use of every serviceable unit of the High Seas Fleet, and of every submarine and Zeppelin available. At dawn on 28 October the armada was to have sailed. Two powerful groups of cruisers and destroyers were to advance simultaneously towards the Flanders coast and the mouth of the Thames, bombarding shore targets and sinking everything they came across. The main fleet was to follow, screened from British submarine attack by swarms of destroyers.

Immediately after news of the sortie had been received, the Grand Fleet, it was anticipated, would emerge from its Scottish bases in full strength and steam south at high speed to intercept the enemy. But its path would be strewn with invisible traps. Lines of U-boats would be lying in ambush athwart the course of the fleet. It would also have to pass through the huge cordon of mines, which the *UC* submarines had planted off the Firth of Tay, and, further to the south, through five more mine barriers, containing 1,500 mines, which were to be laid by five fast German cruisers on the day preceding the sortie.

The U-boats were to be arranged on the well-tried method that had once before caused Admiral Jellicoe to report that he had 'run into a hell of U-boats.' (This was in August 1916, during a half-hearted sortie by the German fleet, when the Grand Fleet sighted numerous enemy submarines and lost the light cruisers *Falmouth* and *Nottingham* from this cause.) As an additional guarantee against surprise, twelve Zeppelins were to scout for the fleet, the embargo on their employment in the North Sea area having been lifted for this special occasion.

Finally, the entire force of German torpedo boats was to be hurled against the Grand Fleet during the night of its advance, the captains having orders to sacrifice their craft if necessary, and to get within torpedo range at all costs. Then, when the Grand Fleet had been decimated and demoralised by these repeated attacks, it was to be engaged off Terschelling by the German battle squadrons at full strength.

An important feature of the general plan were raids by cruisers and destroyers on shipping in the Downs and the Thames estuary. The Germans believed we were preparing to throw an army into Holland, with the object of attacking the army group of Crown Prince Rupprecht from the rear and cutting off his retreat. They hoped, therefore, to come upon the transports assembled for this expedition and send them to the bottom.

Secret instructions from the naval staff impressed upon the commanding officer of every German vessel the absolute necessity for the most vigorous and ruthless action. The 'safety first' principle that hitherto had governed all operations was to be discarded. Ships and men were to be expended without hesitation to exploit any promising situation, and in every case fire was to be opened without making any recognition signal, since the sortie was so carefully organised that any craft sighted was practically certain to be an enemy. If it were not, so much the worse for the unlucky neutral or friend.

As we have seen, this plan, so impressive on paper, was built up on a number of false assumptions. In the first place, the gigantic minefield off the Firth of Tay, which was expected to sink or cripple many of the best British battleships, had been quietly removed by our sweepers. Secondly, the presence of U-boat ambuscades on the Grand Fleet's line of advance was taken for granted, and measures were concerted to evade them. Thirdly, we knew beforehand that five German cruisers were to steal across the North Sea to lay additional mine barriers just before the great sortie, and we had arranged for them to be intercepted and destroyed by an overwhelming force long before they reached the points at which their deadly cargoes were to be jettisoned. Fourthly, the Harwich Force and the Dover Patrol had both been warned, and neither would have been caught unprepared, if caught at all. Fifthly, special arrangements were made for the protection of shipping in the Downs, and all cross-Channel transport sailings were to be suspended at the first sign of a move by the enemy.

In the Grand Fleet, everything was in readiness for 'The Day'. Since Jutland the fleet itself had been strongly reinforced by new vessels of every type, and also by six American battleships under Admiral Rodman. All capital ships had been fitted with devices that reduced the danger of magazine explosions to the minimum, and many had received additional armour protection. Gunnery had improved, and the new armour-piercing shells made it certain that every hit would be effective. All vessels were equipped with paravanes, enabling them to pass through minefields with comparative impunity, while special destroyer flotillas, carrying high-speed paravanes, could steam ahead of the fleet and blaze a safe trail for it through any mine-infested zone.

The Grand Fleet was well provided with aircraft, including many fighters and torpedo planes. The former would unquestionably have given the Zeppelin scouts a rough handling; the torpedo planes would have been launched against the enemy's battle fleet as soon as it was sighted.

In his evidence before the Reichstag Committee Admiral von Trotha, expatiating on the merits of the plan, said: 'The advantage lay with the Germans, since the High Seas Fleet would have had to advance only 150 miles, and the cruisers, for their attack in the Channel, the same distance, while the British Grand Fleet would have had to travel 400 miles from Scapa Flow.' That would have been true had the sortie caught us napping; but we were, in fact, forewarned. Consequently, the Grand Fleet would have left its bases much earlier than the Germans anticipated, and the latter would have found themselves brought to action at a time and place chosen by Admiral Beatty, not by the German naval staff.

That the light flotillas told off to raid the Channel would have been cut off and exterminated is beyond dispute, having regard to the reception that had been prepared for them. That the Zeppelins could have given the German Commander-in-Chief timely warning of the Grand Fleet's approach is highly improbable, in view of the number of British aeroplanes detailed to look out for and attack the hostile airships. Again, the knowledge we had of the U-boat traps, and the efficiency of our paravane gear, would very probably have saved the Grand Fleet from serious loss through torpedoes or mines. Finally, we knew of the intended mass attack by German destroyers during the night, and did not fear it, since our night-fighting organisation had been improved enormously since Jutland. Moreover, since the Germans in all likelihood would place our fleet some 200 miles further north than it actually was, their destroyers would have very little chance of finding it.

The prospect was, therefore, that the Grand Fleet would arrive on the scene long before it was expected, and engage the High Seas Fleet with a two-to-one superiority. It was the enemy, not ourselves, who would be caught unawares. On the British side, every man in the fleet would have been thirsting for battle, for at no time had there been the slightest depreciation of discipline or fighting spirit. On the German side the lower-deck personnel, grown stale through years of confinement in harbour, seething with discontent, and openly at variance with its officers, would suddenly have discovered the deathtrap into which it had been led under false pretences. None can tell what would have happened in these circumstances, but to infer that the Germans would have fought rather less gamely than they did at Jutland is not unreasonable. Be that as it may, the result of an action fought to a finish under the conditions here depicted would scarcely have been in doubt. Humanly speaking, a German victory was impossible. At best, a sorely battered remnant of the High Seas Fleet might have limped back to port, but the virtual destruction of the whole force was confidently awaited by British and American flag-officers, who knew not only the preparations we had made, but almost every detail of the German 'secret' plan. For that knowledge they were largely indebted to the naval intelligence department.

But the great sortie never took place. In spite of every precaution, the secret leaked out. According to several accounts, suspicion was first aroused on the lower deck by the indiscreet conduct of the younger officers in openly toasting 'The Day' while they were at mess, this being reported to the men by the wardroom stewards. Meanwhile the date of sailing had been altered to 30 October. On the evening of the 29th, therefore, all ships were ordered to raise steam. It was given out that the fleet was to make a short cruise in the Bight; nothing was said even of a possible encounter with the enemy.

By this time, however, the men were convinced that their lives were to be wantonly sacrificed for the personal glory of their officers. Leaflets to this effect had been privily distributed throughout the fleet, urging the men not to allow themselves to be driven to the shambles. As Prince Max of Baden has since pointed out in his memoirs, 'the naval leaders, whose business it was to make as certain of their morale as their material forces before seeking a decisive action, had planned their undertaking at the worst possible moment, when the armistice negotiations were in progress and a hundred false hopes were being raised in the people. Their scheme was inevitably doomed to failure in face of the men's feeling that, as peace was about to be concluded, it was senseless to go and get themselves killed.'

The order to raise steam appears to have been obeyed in most of the ships, if not in all. But on the same evening a majority of the men in the battleships *Thüringen* and *Markgraf* refused to stand their night watches, and went to their hammocks, from which in the morning they refused to turn out. Cases of insubordination occurred in other ships, and in view of this development the Commander-in-Chief, Admiral von Hipper, wisely cancelled the signal to put to sea.

During 30 October the atmosphere in the fleet was charged with electricity. Towards evening the storm broke. The scene in the *Thüringen* has been graphically described by one of her officers:

As though by agreement, the men came streaming from all parts
of the ship – gun crews, stokers, and lower-deck parties – to the
forward battery, where they prepared to resist. Hawsers were cut
through, the weighing of the anchors was rendered impossible, and
the electric light was cut off, so that order could not be restored. A
grim, uncouth horde of men shut themselves up forward from the
rest of the ship. The officers armed themselves, and mounted guard
over the after part of the ship to protect vital compartments and
gear against attack by the mutineers.

The mutiny in the *Thüringen* was temporarily suppressed by
the calling up of a destroyer and a submarine, which took station on the beam with orders to fire torpedoes into the ship
unless the men returned to duty by a given time. This they did,
whereupon a number were placed under arrest and sent ashore.
There, however, the armed escort refused to proceed further,
and fraternised with the prisoners, who broke away and roamed
through the streets of Kiel, waving red flags and singing revolutionary songs. Meanwhile the mutiny had spread to other ships.
Very soon the whole fleet was in open revolt. Strangely enough,
scarcely any resistance was offered by the officers, most of whom
stood aside while their men hauled down the ensign and ran
up the red flag in its place. Only in the battleship *Koenig* did a
handful of officers attempt to oppose force by force. In that ship
the commanding officer, Captain Weniger, was badly wounded
in trying to defend the colours, while two of his officers were
shot dead at his side.

The fact that the mutiny originated in the big ships shows
very clearly the demoralising effect of prolonged service in harbour. Among the crews of the destroyers, which had put in

much more time at sea, the revolt spread more slowly, and the submarine personnel remained loyal almost to the last. But by 3 November the High Seas Fleet had ceased to exist as a fighting entity. Discipline had gone to pieces; the ships were being run by 'Soviets', and most of the officers were ashore or confined to their cabins. Not even the publication of the armistice terms, which demanded *inter alia* the surrender of the fleet to the Allies, sufficed to reawaken the fighting spirit of the men. There was, it is true, some talk of 'resisting to the last', but the personnel as a whole regarded the impending humiliation of their service with indifference.

A fortnight later the German battle fleet, escorted by the Grand Fleet, steamed into the Firth of Forth, and eventually was remanded to Scapa Flow in custody, there to await the Allies' decision as to its fate. It is unnecessary to repeat here the well-known details of that historic event, or of the subsequent sinking of the vessels by their own crews. The world's comment at the time was scathing enough, as was but natural; but after the lapse of so many years it would be a sorry task to dwell upon the abasement of an enemy who, in almost every action at sea, fought with courage and tenacity. The officers and men who took the German ships into action at Jutland, Coronel, and the Falklands will always be held in honour by British seamen.

By the end of the war the naval intelligence division had grown to imposing dimensions, as a reference to the 'Navy List' of December 1918 will show. Its staff included experts on every branch of naval affairs; linguists who between them were masters of practically every modern language, European and Asiatic, and of not a few ancient tongues to boot; cryptographers to whom almost every code was an open book, and chemists who not only knew all about secret inks, but could even reconstruct a complete document from a handful of ashes taken out of a stove. In fact, the ID of that period might be said to represent a galaxy of practitioners in all the esoteric arts. Most of them held commissions in the Royal Navy, the Royal Marines, the Royal Naval Volunteer Reserve, or the Royal Naval Reserve, but there was a minority of members who, for one reason or another, preferred to remain civilians, and these, if the least conspicuous, were by no means the least useful units of the vast organisation.

A complete record of ID work and achievements during the war period would run into many volumes, and form a story more thrilling, we believe, than any of the histories on other aspects of the great struggle that have yet appeared. But it is a record that will never be printed, because no state, however liberal-minded, can afford to reveal the whole of its arcana. Nor would it be in the public interest to disclose the whole truth about our secret service operations even during the very period when they were most completely justified. Since perpetual peace is not yet assured, a time may come when the safety of the realm may once more necessitate an inquisition into the designs of its enemies, actual and potential, and the mechanism of intelligence that functioned so admirably in the past may have to be set in motion again. That is one reason why it would be improper to divulge ID methods in greater detail, and for the same reason we have preferred to write this narrative in outline, leaving the informed few to dot the 'i's and cross the 't's for their own satisfaction.

But we have said enough to convey a sufficiently clear and comprehensive idea of what the naval secret service accomplished, and enough, we hope and believe, to vindicate the memory of those who served England valiantly, though in silence and an obscurity from which they themselves prefer not to emerge. They were the men who, at the call of duty, went forth on perilous emprise to 'search, seek, find out'; who toiled unceasingly to discover and circumvent the plots that were laid for the undoing of their country. Their task is done, and their most fervent wish is that it may never have to be resumed, either in their own lifetime or in that of any succeeding generation.